ARE YOU READY FOR COMMERCIAL REAL ESTATE?

12 Things Every Small Business Owner Should Know

Cathy Criado

Second Edition, Revised and Updated, published in 2025

Cathy Criado

First Edition published in 2016.

ISBN: 978-0-9971545-3-5

Printed in the United States of America.

ARE YOU READY FOR COMMERCIAL REAL ESTATE?

12 Things Every Small Business Owner Should Know

By Cathy Criado

A LOVE NOTE FROM MY MOM

My mother bought me this beautiful book as a gift many years ago, pre-children. I love this life outlook so am sharing with you too.

Each new day is an opportunity to start all over again... to cleanse our minds and hearts anew and to clarify our vision. And let us not clutter up today with the leavings of other days.

Apples of Gold by Jo Petty

DEDICATION

This book is dedicated to my parents. My mom gives me encouragement, love, and support, personally and professionally. She's a beautiful woman, inside and out who is always willing to forgive. Thank heaven for unconditional love and moms.

My dad learned to become the good dad that he was and a source of strength and enlightenment for me. He once told me he wasn't worried about me or my career; "Doll, you have perseverance and smarts and I'll bet on that over just smarts any day." He was an excellent writer so when I feel writer's block or need to be particularly technical, I wear a pencil tucked into my ear like he used to do when writing, or thinking, to call on his spirit now that he's gone.

ACKNOWLEDGEMENTS

To all my family, friends, and clients that have trusted me with their business and referrals. I value, love and appreciate you!

To Prof. Palani-Rajan Kadapakkam, Ph.D. For making me realize that there's no point in being in business if I don't want to understand business from a number's perspective.

To Prof. Mark W. Phillips, Ph.D. You opened my eyes to the practical aspect of consulting with your Tabasco story and others. Real world is so important and necessary to be an effective consultant.

To Prof. LJ Shrum, Ph.D. You made me feel like I was the smartest person in the room when you called on me to explain complex Consumer Behavior theory models when nobody else seemed to understand them. Confidence comes from trust and integrity, which you encourage.

INTRODUCTION

WHY I WROTE THIS BOOK

Everything I know about business and real estate came from equal parts education, experience, and curiosity — through my studies at The University of Texas at Arlington (B.B.A.), The University of Texas at San Antonio (M.B.A.), earning my Real Estate Broker license from the Texas Real Estate Commission, and completing countless transactions along the way.

I didn't come from wealth or a business-minded family. My parents weren't college educated, and I didn't know anyone who owned a business until my 20s. It still amazes me that in a country based on capitalism and entrepreneurship, that so many Americans grow up without understanding business, credit, or our monetary system.

My awakening came during graduate school at UT San Antonio. I had returned to school after years as a full-time mom — raising my children, one with special needs — while working as an Office Manager at a chiropractic clinic, a Travel Agency Manager, and a consultant for a children's educational book company. I enjoyed helping people, but I felt stifled. I wanted to use my brain more, engage my critical thinking skills, and dive into business strategy. That M.B.A. empowered me to do exactly that.

We studied businesses the way you dissect frogs in middle school — pulling apart every piece to see how it worked. We analyzed corporations, debated their strategies, and explored why some thrived while others failed. Most of our discussions centered on large companies like General Electric and Cisco Systems, with case studies on leaders like Jack Welch and John Chambers. While those examples were valuable, they felt distant — out of touch with businesses that I could relate to or had experienced.

I felt drawn to research companies like Chick-fil-A and Hobby Lobby on my own. I wanted to understand how they started, what made them grow, and why people were so passionate about them. Their success wasn't just about chicken or crafts — it was about philosophy, purpose, and leadership. That's when I discovered my passion for entrepreneurial enterprises and alternative business models.

During my senior year, I took a marketing strategy course with Dr. L.J. Shrum, the Department Chair, that connected classroom theory with real-world consulting. We worked with local businesses — a wedding event company and a roofing company — to implement marketing plans, study pricing, and reposition their services. That course was the spark that ignited my love for business consulting.

Later, with Dr. Phillips, I learned one of the most valuable lessons I still share with clients today: most startups don't fail just because of cash flow challenges — they fail because owners treat their business like their baby. Nobody wants to hear their baby isn't perfect. I call it *Ugly Baby Syndrome.*

TIP: *Always ask for objective, third-party feedback and be willing to hear what you need to hear, not just what you want to hear. That's where real growth happens.*

I follow that philosophy. When I have new ideas for branding, marketing, etc. I run my ideas through a Mastermind group and ask clients for feedback after every transaction. Most feedback is great, but sometimes I miss the mark. It's not always easy to hear, but those insights help me refine, improve, and strengthen my strategies moving forward.

After graduate school, I completed an internship helping to launch The Staubach Company's San Antonio, Texas office, which has since been acquired by a large, national firm. I then joined a commercial real estate and development firm that specialized in retail shopping centers. That experience gave me hands-on insight into engineering, design, and construction — knowledge that continues to serve my clients who want to build their own projects.

Then came the 2008 financial crisis, and like so many in our industry, I had to pivot. Development halted, so I shifted into residential and bank-owned properties, mastering short sales and foreclosures. That chapter added to my understanding of market cycles and resilience.

Over time, I began focusing on Small Business Owners — helping them launch, reorganize, expand, or even close strategically when necessary. I built a brokerage team that grew to more than a dozen agents, but I eventually realized that mentoring agents wasn't my calling. My passion is helping Small Business Owners build their dreams and legacies.

Today, I'm branded simply as **Criado Realty** because people choose me for *me*, not a company name. My value goes far beyond closing transactions. My education, experience, and strategic mindset allow me to help clients see real estate as a business tool — a way to create stability, opportunity, and generational wealth.

A business coach once told me, "You need to write a book — you explain things creatively." I tried to find something similar to my commercial real estate philosophy, but nothing existed. Realizing that there was an opportunity, in 2016, I wrote and self-published *Are You Ready for Commercial Real Estate*? No ghostwriter. No consultant. Just me, a self-imposed deadline, and a passion to share my philosophy and strategies. It was imperfect — like many first editions — but it was mine.

Years later, with far more experience and perspective, I knew it was time to do it better. This Second Edition is better organized, more practical, and richer in real-world examples. Think of it as having me by your side — walking you through every decision, helping you ask the right questions, and empowering you to think like a Small Business Owner when it comes to real estate.

You still need an experienced Agent — but at least now you have a written version of me to guide you. You are always welcome to take it a step further and contact me for consulting, collaborating, and helping you make your next strategic move.

www.CathyCriado.com

WHAT YOU'LL GAIN FROM THIS BOOK

Becoming a Small Business Owner is a lot like parenting. *You build it, nurture it, grow it, then retire it, and hopefully you don't kill it. The difference is, when you have children, you can find books and advice on everything from pregnancy to growing healthy adults.*

When you start a business, that kind of guidance is much harder to find, much less finding real estate or blogs for making prudent lease vs. buy or thinking beyond just brick and mortar. That's why I wrote this book. After years of working with Small Business Owners, I saw the need for a clear, practical guide to help them make smarter real estate decisions — the kind that support their business rather than burden it.

Commercial real estate decisions are far more complex than the old saying *"Location, Location, Location."* While most Small Business Owners think of real estate as an expense, I challenge you to look at it differently. Your property should sit squarely in the *asset* column, mentally and physically. It's more than just brick and mortar — it's a business tool, a growth vehicle, and in many cases, a valuable branding statement. My hope is that this book helps you see real estate through that lens — and gives you the tools to make the best, most informed decisions possible.

This book is designed to make you rethink the function of real estate — to see how it can *leverage* your business, not sink it. Inside this book I'll share strategic insights, both qualitative and quantitative, to help you evaluate whether leasing, buying, or building is the right move for you.

I approach every engagement as a business consultant who happens to specialize in real estate. My goal is to fully understand your current and future needs so we can create strategies that fit, including your eventual exit plan — because every smart business decision starts with the end in mind.

A strong business plan is essential. You should always know your 3-, 5-, and 10-year goals because real estate is rarely a short-term decision. Most investments extend at least three years, often five or ten, and even longer for capital-intensive operations or property ownership.

To guide you through that process, I've included several proprietary tools I developed for my clients:

- **S.M.A.R.T. Decision Planner** – to help you structure your goals and priorities.
- **FinancialWise Planner** – to align financial stability with your real estate strategy.
- **TimeWise Planner** – to plan the necessary steps to achieve your plans.
- **EcoWise Guide** – to integrate sustainability and long-term efficiency into your business decisions and do it in a business savvy manor.

As one of my clients, Jorge Herrera, CPA, CIA, often says:

"Are you ready to rock and roll?"

TABLE OF CONTENTS

	Dedication	
	Acknowledgements	
	Introduction	
Chapter 1	Understanding Commercial Real Estate	1
Chapter 2	Shopping for your Broker	17
Chapter 3	Shopping for a Property from the Property Centric Perspective	25
Chapter 4	Shopping for Property from the End-User Centric Perspective	31
Chapter 5	FinancialWise	39
Chapter 6	Lease vs. Buy and Why	47
Chapter 7	Negotiations and Contracts	53
Chapter 8	Leasing Basics	59
Chapter 9	Buying and Building	71
Chapter 10	SMART Decision Planner	77
Chapter 11	TimeWise Planner	83
Chapter 12	EcoWise Decisions	85
	About the Author	
	12 Favorite Business Books	

CHAPTER ONE

UNDERSTANDING COMMERCIAL REAL ESTATE

Commercial real estate use can be complex, especially with revitalization and mixed-use zonings. In chapter one I will define what it is, its history and trends, classifications, and valuation from the market viewpoint and the appraisal viewpoint. Both are valuations but differing by the Small Business Owner and a licensed valuation party (or third party).

DEFINING COMMERCIAL REAL ESTATE

The clearest differential between Commercial and Residential Real Estate is that one is financially-driven while the other is emotionally-driven. Here is the expanded explanation.

COMMERCIAL REAL ESTATE

This property is intended for business operations or for income-producing purposes. It includes office buildings, retail centers, industrial facilities, hotels, and multifamily properties of four or more units. It also includes unimproved and improved land. Its core objective is to produce l income and/or capital appreciation sometimes referred to buy and hold to increase over time even if the income does not currently cover all of the cost of ownership.

RESIDENTIAL REAL ESTATE

This property is intended for personal residence(s) i.e. single-family homes, townhomes, condominiums, and duplexes or triplexes. These assets are designed for personal occupancy and make up the largest segment of the real estate market. However, some residential uses are handled as commercial for financing. A portfolio of residential would be financed as commercial.

There is some gray area sometimes, that comes down to use vs. scale and ownership. For example, a condo project may sit in a mixed-use or commercial zone and still require a commercial construction loan—even though the finished units are residential.

COMMERCIAL REAL ESTATE PAST AND PRESENT

The world has been dominated by Mixed-use environments until modern times. Walking was the primary mode of transportation with the occasional horse, camel, or other animal assistance. Buildings were not zoned or classified; they were just buildings that Small Business Owners built to run their operations. It was pretty common to sell things from their house too. The industrial revolution created a need for centralizing real estate for business. The walkability scale became essential.

The Industrialization Age, mass pollution issues, and the mass influx of factory workers, domestic housing boomed. Mass migration to rural areas developed thus beginning the separation of land use.

In the 1920s, the U.S. National Zoning Enabling Act of 1923 and a series of National Subdivision and Planning acts in English-speaking countries first set forth standards and practices of single-use zoning to be adopted by every municipality, which soon became the standard for all post-World War II development. These laws enforced and codified standards for modern suburban design as it is known today, which have been exported to many other countries through planning professionals and transportation engineers.

Prior to WWII, that's how most of the United States zoning was planned. The arrival of mass transit systems and more so with the private automobile (and cheap oil), Developers started to build distant, self-sustaining communities. Factor in the Baby Boomers and the age of the Suburbs the face of real estate changed.

While the first official (enclosed) shopping mall recorded was opened in Southdale Center in Edina, Minnesota (USA), opened October 8, 1956, **it was the 1960's that the Malling of America emerged**. Downtowns became Ghost Towns. Malls began to proliferate changing the urban core of most American cities.

In the 80's a surge of High Rise (Sky Scraper) offices, apartments, and large retail shopping centers (Power Centers) once again changed real estate; it effected where people chose to live and residential Developers pivoted. These architectural landscape changes created the death of "downtown" and inner cities by the 1970's, but has resurged in alternative uses.

Commercial Development is interesting from an influence perspective; it seems that most Developers today talk about "roof tops" and build commercially to support residential needs i.e. shopping centers. They think they are chasing roof tops. But are they? Residential Developers build according to land availability and utility lines, but so do Commercial Developers. If they build a large-scale office park or data center, they also need residential and retail nearby to support the workforce. Which influences which? It is more symbiotic than either Developer gives credit.

Gentrification has spurred New Urbanism, which is an urban planning movement focused on human-scaled design, walkable neighborhoods, mixed-use development, and community engagement as an alternative to post-WWII urban sprawl. Its goal is to reform real estate development by fostering balanced development of housing and jobs, promoting transit-oriented design, increasing social equity and environmental sustainability, and creating a high quality of life through walkable, interconnected, and human-scaled communities.

I appreciate Developers meeting consumer needs. I also appreciate responsible Developers who consider the social, ethical, financial, and sustainable standpoint. As Martha Stewart says, "It's a good thing." Without Developers making retailing and work place solutions convenient perhaps our lives would be more about commuting than quality time. That is an issue in many major cities today, especially California and New York, which is resulting in mass relocations to Texas and Florida (besides the politics and affordability).

COMMERCIAL REAL ESTATE CLASSIFICATIONS

Basic knowledge of real estate classifications will help you understand what can be used for what and to avoid having use crises by knowing and performing Due Diligence.

I mention Due Diligence frequently throughout this book since it is the cause of many real estate failures. Years ago, I was able to obtain a super deal for a Buyer Client. There was this Retail Condominium available for a discount because that Small Business Owner failed to research the Covenants, Codes, and Restrictions (CCRs) of a property he had purchased directly from the Developer without a real estate broker, which had a use restriction. They only allowed one restaurant within the complex even if not the same cuisine. I saw this opportunity and was able to help my dental client capitalize on his loss. Do your Due Diligence.

Most cities define the property use and these codes do change occasionally. Just because you see an auto garage shop doesn't mean that you can build a car wash next door. Zoning changes are not automatically grandfathered. Some cities have Master Plans, while others do not and those are then case by case approvals to build.

OFFICE

Office is typically used by law firms, real estate practices, financial planners, insurance services, etcetera. Types include Garden Offices, Low Rise, High Rise, Condominiums, Office Parks, and Creative Space. They can also go into Flex Space. Medical Offices are usually treated differently due to plumbing needs and some Landlords want to keep medical away due to wellness concerns for general office users.

RETAIL

Retail is all about foot traffic and demographics. Retail is usually more expensive than Office as it requires the highest level of visibility, traffic counts, parking, and signage. Some Office users may benefit too such as real estate offices, insurance offices, or military recruiting offices to capitalize on the walk-in traffic. Retail includes Power Centers, Neighborhood Centers, Strip Centers, Free Standing Pad Sites, and Retail Condominiums. Very commonly the Free-Standing Pads are drive through businesses like restaurants or those that need customized builds.

INDUSTRIAL

Industrial real estate refers to commercial properties specifically designed and used for manufacturing, warehousing, storage, and distribution of goods. These specialized buildings often feature functional elements like high ceilings, loading docks, reinforced floors, and dedicated space for heavy machinery, catering to the needs of businesses in the supply chain by providing the infrastructure to produce and transport products.

Flexible use: refers to commercial properties specifically designed and used for industrial activities, but can be flexible about its use such as a fitness studio, photography business, or other destination type business that wants lower rent rates and does not benefit by walking traffic.

MULTIFAMILY

A multifamily property is residential use real estate containing multiple separate, independent living units within a complex, i.e. as apartments, condominiums, or townhomes. These units typically have their own private entrances and facilities, though they may share common areas and amenities like hallways, laundry rooms, or a yard. Commonly Investors refer size by "doors" not units.

SPECIAL USE

Anything that is non-conforming such as a church, sports arena/court, assisted living, zoo, event center, hospital, etcetera.
End-Users sometimes may go down in zoning but not usually up without re-zoning. Meaning, an insurance company could lease or buy an old warehouse to repurpose as Creative Office space. However, a manufacturer, especially if uses box trucks or chemicals, might not be allowed to repurpose an Office Park without going through the re-zoning process. Commercial trucks, welding, and chemicals have a negative environmental footprint that general office or a shoe store would not have. Zoning takes into account environmental factors and traffic impact on a community.

UNDERSTANDING MARKET VALUE

Commercial Real Estate value is like people's opinions; everyone has one but none of them are fact. One might argue that a third-party appraisal by a licensed appraiser is fact, but it still an Opinion of Value and the real or true value lies with the benefit of the Small Business Owner or Investor.

What is the *true* Market Value?

COUNTY APPRAISAL VALUE

Consumers typically think this value has merit; it does, but only as it pertains to taxation. The County Appraisal Districts do not have access to the property information necessary to give it a correct valuation. It is the least accurate.

END-USER VALUE

The End-User could be the property owner or a tenant. The one who gets the most value is subject to the type of business operating from the property, the valuation of the community, or other factors. There could be a rocks and minerals stores making a modest living, or a doctor making a considerable income, or the property could be in an area where a new Microsoft Data plant is being built causing property values to increase well above average. While the property owner may be charging affordable rental rates, when those leases expire surely the rates will increase or might possibly sell the property for a higher or best use. There are many variables in this valuation.

BROKER PRICE OPINION (BPO)

BPOs are commonly performed but are not as accurate or reliable as a Licensed Appraiser Valuation. Typically, a BPO is comparison based and many Brokers are not knowledgeable about financial calculations. Look for a Broker who has completed a certified commercial sales training class and knowledge about the area and industry type.

LICENSED APPRAISER VALUATION

An Appraiser may offer valid facts about the property's "Comparison Approach" or the "Income Approach" valuation based on financial history or opportunity. This can be a certified number, but still, this is not the *true* market real value.

MARKET VALUE DEFINITION

The *true market value* is what a Buyer is *willing and able* to pay and a Seller is *willing and able* to accept.

Let's look at a little scenario. 1234 Main St is on the market and zoned C3 for office, retail, or light industrial/flex. The structure is a 1905 building that formerly was a government dignitary home with some local history and charm. It is located on a high traffic street with good visibility. The county appraised it for $395,000. The Licensed Appraiser valued it at $485,000 based on its current use as a dental office. The list price is $475,000, debt free. The property is currently making $50,000 mo. ($600,000 per year net income from the practice).

Mr. Moneybags, wants to convert it back to its 1960's use, a quadplex dwelling. He is expecting to make enough income to get a desirable return on investment at $425,000 including another $100,000 for renovations and repairs, so is only willing to pay $425,000.

Dr. Lovescandy, wants to use it as a dental practice and needs the Nitrous Oxide system valued at $150,000 and the customers from the former dentist, so she is willing to pay $475,000.

Mr. Moneybags can do a quick close, as-is condition, cash. Dr. Lovescandy needs 60 days to close on an SBA loan and will do an inspection. **What is the value? Which one would you sell to and why?**

HIGHEST AND BEST USE

Most Developers and Investors evaluate a property's full potential using this approach as it takes in much more consideration than just data or financial analysis. It looks at the biggest picture. Revisiting the 1905 property, here is an application of Highest and Best.

A Medical Office is likely the Highest and Best Use of the property since Medical Office build-out has considerable expenses and tear out to install plumbing (gas is plumbing). To tear it out might seem wasteful.

However, a third buyer, Buyer C wants to tear it down to build an outdoor micro-brewery and eatery. Buyer C wants it to build an event venue with a café. Depending on the market trends of the area and changing demographics the decisions and value is varied. Is it being gentrified? Is it a dying area? Really, any of these uses could be equally or more valuable depending on the demand for that business in that geographic area and with those demographic trends.

This valuation analysis is provided to help Small Business Owners like you to understand what a Seller might be thinking when he receives your offer. Knowing these factors will strengthen your negotiation power considerably.

There are three widely accepted valuations from third party Appraisers; Comparison, Income, and Replacement. In real estate we only consider the first two. Replacement is how insurance companies value.

TIP: *Keep in mind that you need to prove the replacement value to get the best outcome. Keep records of improvements, maintenance, and take annual photographs to negotiate your best valuation.*

LICENSED APPRAISER VALUATION METHODS

COMPARISON METHOD

Most commonly used in Residential, but may be used to compare two or more properties that have like features. Adjustments (+/-) are made for the differences, which is a dollar per square foot rate applied to the subject property. If the property is vacant and has no income history this might be applied, however, future income opportunity could also be considered if it can be verified, such as a nearby apartment complex to an existing apartment complex.

INCOME METHOD

There are several financial models that can be applied and I would suggest that you familiarize yourself because your banker or accountant might ask these kinds of questions when considering your financing. I will cover the three most common models: Cash on Cash, Internal Rate of Return, and Cap Rate.

CASH ON CASH

The Cash-on-cash return is a metric used to measure the annual pre-tax cash flow generated by an income-producing property relative to the amount of actual cash an investor has put into it. It helps Investors understand the performance of an investment and is a key metric in real estate. It is an easy to understand and easy to calculate model. Here is the model:

$$\text{Cash-on-Cash Return} = \frac{\text{Annual Pre-Tax Cash Flow}}{\text{Total Cash Invested}}$$

Example: A $3,000,000 property generates $30,000 per month in income ($360,000 per year). $360,000/$3,000,000 yields a 12% Cash on Cash Return on Investment

If the property could yield $30,000 per month but needs $500,000 in repairs additionally, then the Cash-on-Cash ROI would be $360,000/$3,500,000 = 10%.

WHY CASH-ON-CASH RETURN IS A GOOD METRIC

Measures actual cash performance: Unlike other metrics that might focus on a property's overall market value, cash-on-cash return shows how much profit your actual out-of-pocket cash investment is generating each year.

Considers financing: Because it accounts for mortgage payments, this metric is especially useful for evaluating leveraged real estate deals. It allows you to see how your financing strategy impacts your annual cash flow.

Simple and intuitive: The calculation is straightforward, providing a clear and quick snapshot of an investment's annual income performance. It helps you easily compare multiple potential properties.

Evaluates passive income: For buy-and-hold Investors focused on consistent cash flow, this metric helps determine if a property will generate the stable income needed to support their financial goals.

LIMITATIONS OF CASH-ON-CASH RETURN

While valuable, cash-on-cash return has several limitations:

Ignores appreciation: It does not account for the property's potential long-term value increase, which can be a significant source of return for real estate Investors.

Doesn't include tax benefits: The calculation is pre-tax and does not factor in potential tax deductions, such as for depreciation and mortgage interest, which can significantly affect a property's overall profitability.

A single-year snapshot: It provides a look at a property's performance over a single year. It does not consider how cash flow might change over the life of the investment.

Can be skewed by leverage: While it accounts for financing, it can make returns appear artificially high for properties with significant debt, which carries higher risk.

The most widely used valuation is The Capitalization Rate.
The Capitalization Rate, or Cap Rate, is a real estate metric that measures the potential annual rate of return on an income-producing property. It is considered a "good" metric because it is a simple,

standardized way to compare the relative value and risk of different investment properties.

CAPITALIZATON RATE

The Cap Rate is the ratio of a property's annual Net Operating Income (NOI) to its current market value.

- **Net Operating Income (NOI):** This is the property's total annual rental income minus all operating expenses. Operating expenses include property taxes, insurance, and maintenance, but exclude mortgage payments and interest.
- **Current Market Value:** This is the property's appraised value, which may differ from its initial purchase price.

For example, a property with an NOI of \$500,000 and a market value of \$10,000,000 has a Cap Rate of 5% (\$500,000 / \$10,000,000).

$$Cap\ Rate = \frac{Annual\ Net\ Operating\ Income}{Current\ Market\ Value} \times 100$$

Why the Cap Rate is a good metric.
The Cap Rate is a valuable tool for real estate Investors for several key reasons:

- **Easy comparison:** It provides a simple, apples-to-apples way to compare potential returns on different properties, such as a multifamily building and a commercial retail space.
- **Quick risk assessment:** A property's Cap Rate offers insight into its risk profile. A higher Cap Rate often indicates a higher-risk investment with greater potential returns, while a lower Cap Rate typically suggests lower risk and more stable cash flow.

- **Aids in valuation:** By knowing the Cap Rate for similar properties in the market, an investor can use it to estimate a property's value. This is especially useful for a quick evaluation.

- **Focuses on core performance:** Since the calculation excludes financing costs like mortgage payments, it allows Investors to evaluate the property's intrinsic performance based purely on its operations.

Limitations of using Cap Rate. While useful, the Cap Rate has limitations and should not be the sole basis for an investment decision.

- **Doesn't account for debt**: It ignores the impact of financing, which is crucial for most real estate Investors. A high-interest loan could make a high-cap-rate property less profitable.

Doesn't predict growth: The calculation is a snapshot based on the current financial picture and does not factor in future changes, such as potential income growth from renovations or **DEPRECIATION** over time.

- **Not for all properties:** The Cap Rate is most reliable for properties with stable, consistent income, like commercial buildings and long-term rental units. It is less suitable for properties with fluctuating income, such as short-term vacation rentals or flipped homes.

INTERNAL RATE OF RETURN

The IRR is a financial metric used to estimate the profitability of potential investments and projects. It represents the annualized rate of return that makes the net present value (NPV) of all cash flows from a particular investment equal to zero. (There is no model shown because it is not a formula. A spreadsheet is required to run an analysis on all the numbers. Excel has such a template.)

HOW IRR WORKS

At its core, IRR accounts for the time value of money—the concept that a dollar today is worth more than a dollar tomorrow. The IRR calculation works backward from a series of anticipated cash flows to find the discount rate that would make the investment's present value equal to zero.

A project's IRR is then typically compared to a company's minimum required rate of return, also known as the hurdle rate or cost of capital.

- **If IRR > Hurdle Rate:** The project is financially attractive and should be accepted.
- **If IRR < Hurdle Rate:** The project does not meet the minimum return requirements and should be rejected.

YEAR	CASH FLOWS		PV of CASH FLOWS	
0	$	(500,000)	$	(500,000)
1	$	160,000	$	141,247
2	$	160,000	$	124,692
3	$	160,000	$	110,077
4	$	160,000	$	97,176
5	$	500,000	$	26,808
	NPV			**0**
	IRR			**13%**

WHY IRR IS CONSIDERED A GOOD METRIC

Allows for comparison: Because IRR provides a single, standardized percentage, it allows Investors to compare and rank investment opportunities of different sizes and with varying cash flow patterns on an "apples-to-apples" basis.

Considers timing of cash flows: IRR is dynamic and time-sensitive, giving more weight to cash flows that are received sooner. This recognizes that money received earlier can be reinvested to generate additional returns.

Incorporates the time value of money: By discounting future cash flows, IRR provides a more comprehensive and accurate view of an investment's profitability than simpler metrics like Return on Investment (ROI), which do not account for time.

Objective criterion: IRR is a rate of return derived purely from the cash flows of a project, not external market factors. This makes it a neutral and reliable indicator of a project's potential profitability.

LIMITATIONS OF IRR

While a powerful tool, IRR should not be used as the sole deciding metric due to its limitations:

Unrealistic reinvestment assumption: The IRR calculation assumes that all positive cash flows are reinvested at the same rate as the project's IRR. This is often unrealistic, as finding new opportunities with an identical return rate is unlikely. The Modified Internal Rate of Return (MIRR) can address this issue.

Doesn't account for scale: IRR only provides a percentage rate and does not consider the total dollar value of the project. A smaller project might have a higher IRR but yield a smaller total profit than a larger project with a lower IRR.

Can be misleading with irregular cash flows: For projects with cash flows that fluctuate between positive and negative more than once, the IRR formula can sometimes produce multiple results, which can confuse analysis.

Based on forward-looking estimates: IRR relies on projections of future cash flows. If those estimates are inaccurate, the resulting IRR will also be inaccurate, which is particularly relevant in volatile markets.

QUICK REFERENCE TO UNDERSTANDING COMMERCIAL REAL ESTATE

- Defining Commercial
- Commercial Real Estate History and Trends
- Commercial Real Estate Classifications
- Understanding Market Value
- Licensed Appraiser Valuation Approaches

CHAPTER TWO

SHOPPING FOR YOUR BROKER

Knowing how a person becomes licensed and knowing consortiums will help you understand their ability to help you, to understand their expertise, resources, and value. These terms are not equivalent: Real Estate Agent, Broker, and REALTOR. When shopping for your Agent, you should take this into consideration.

Understanding the Difference Between Licensed Real Estate Brokers and Agents

LICENSING REGULATIONS AND RULES

All states require a license to transact third party sales and most require it to perform property management. The criteria vary by state, and twelve states also require an attorney; not Texas. The exam for the license is composed of a National exam and a State exam. The license issued is a Licensed Real Estate Agent (LREA) also known as a "Salesperson." Once they serve this apprenticeship or basic level of licensing, they can do additional education and apply their experience to pursue the Licensed Real Estate Broker (LREB). In my opinion, LREB matters because it's a commitment to the industry, professional development, and demonstrates knowledge, proficiency, and expertise. The licensing for residential and commercial are the same; although I think I think these should be different licenses and criteria. For now, though, it is the additional training and expertise that creates the differentiation.

Throughout this book I reference "Agent," for both the LREA and LREB, unless I specifically mean one or the other. I use "Broker" to refer to the company, not an individual. Agents are Independent

Contractors, not employees so the Broker has limited control over the Agent's actions and processes.

Not All Agents are REALTORS. The public often uses the term REALTOR instead of real estate mostly because the National Association of Realtors promotes the brand. They are not the same.

The National Association of Realtors (NAR) was formed to improve professionalism and to bring real estate agents together to improve marketing efficiency. There is some benefit for Commercial Real Estate Agents such as professional development and access to MLS commercial, unimproved, tear downs for development, farm and ranch and residential to build portfolio opportunities.

An Agent can choose to be a NAR member or not, and typically they also join the state and local board too, and can join more than one per their credentials. The Multiple Listing Service (MLS) was created by local boards to syndicate listings and to replace the antiquated system of the hand written paper notebooks. Residential Agents need to join NAR, et al, to gain access to the MLS and receive industry trends, information, and education. Some Agents join the Commercial division but most join other organizations that allows for connectivity or collaboration.

Being a REALTOR® is useful in many cases since commonly properties are Mixed-use or can easily change from Commercial to Residential, and vice versa. Your Agent may need to know both Commercial and Residential depending on the type of property you are pursing. These are some aspects that the Small Business Owner should consider when searching for their Agent.

AGENCY

Forty two states are Dual Agency, meaning, an Agent has the legal authority to represent both sides of the transaction. It blows my mind because I do not understand how you can be a fiduciary to both. As they say, it is what it is. In Texas, and seven other states, we are "Non-

Dual Agency," meaning, for a specific transaction, an Agent may represent only the Seller/Landlord or the Buyer/Tenant.

All 50 states have an agency disclosure that outlines the basic role of the Seller/Landlord, the Buyer/Tenant, and Intermediary. Intermediary is when two Agents from the same company represent in the same transaction, regardless of fiduciary. They may be sponsored or by the same brokerage but often don't even know the other Agent, given some Brokerages have thousands of Agents. Regardless of what state you reside, it's important to request the Agency Disclosure and ask for an explanation to understand who represents whom.

The **Buyer/Tenant Representation Agreement** is a written document that formally establishes a **fiduciary relationship**—a legal and ethical obligation of trust.

Now, let's talk about what *fiduciary* really means.

A fiduciary is someone who holds a position of trust and acts in the best interest of another person or entity. This relationship is **confidential, binding, and enduring**—it doesn't just end when the paperwork does.

In real estate, we use the mnemonic **OLD CAR** to remember the key fiduciary duties.

FIDUCIARY

O: Obedience means that the Agent follows the lawful instructions of the Client. It's not about what the Agent wants — it's about what the Client wants, as long as those directions are legal and ethical. The Agent's role is to guide, advise, and present options, but ultimately, the Client makes the decisions.

L: Loyalty means the Agent's duty is to the Client — not the Seller, not the Inspector, or Builder. A loyal Agent protects the Client's best interests at all times, even when others involved in the transaction may have competing priorities. When working with multiple Clients, loyalty also means respecting the order in which each relationship began — much like the accounting principle FIFO (First In, First Out). Each Client deserves the same commitment, transparency, and fairness, guided by the timeline and trust established from the start.

D: Disclosure means the Agent must share everything known or discovered about the property that could affect the Client's decision. Transparency isn't optional — it's essential. This duty ensures the Client can make fully informed choices based on accurate and complete information. It's also one of the key reasons the Agency Disclosure exists: to make sure everyone understands who the Agent represents and where their loyalty and duties lie.

C: Confidentiality is the cornerstone of trust in a fiduciary relationship. Anything shared between the Client and Agent is to be held in confidence — before, during, and long after the transaction — essentially, for life. You should be able to trust your Agent's ethics, skill, and professionalism to protect your private information at all times. A true professional knows that confidentiality doesn't expire when the deal closes; it's part of the ongoing trust that defines great representation.

A: Accountability means the Agent is responsible for keeping the Client informed and updated throughout the property search and transaction process. Communication should be timely, accurate, and proactive — not reactive. A great Agent doesn't wait for the Client to ask what's happening; they stay ahead of the curve, providing updates, documentation, and explanations as the process unfolds. Accountability builds confidence — and that's the foundation of every successful client relationship.

R: Reasonable Care and Due Diligence mean your Agent must use their experience, training, and judgment to protect your best interests throughout the transaction. What you don't know *can* hurt you — financially and even physically. Knowing what to research is just as important as knowing how to research it. But if you're not experienced in real estate, you may not even know what questions to ask. That's why it's so important to work with an experienced, smart, and accessible Agent — someone who understands the process, anticipates risks, and takes the steps necessary to help you make safe, informed decisions.

FACTORS TO CONSIDER WHEN CHOOSING YOUR BROKER

Pay Now or Pay More Later

This what my brother Manuel said when I asked him, a personal injury attorney, about seeking out a corporate attorney regarding a business matter. Similarly, when you hire a top-notch Agent, you might pay a bit more than if you just hired a friend — but hiring the right person makes the difference in your return on investment (ROI). The right Agent can save you far more than what you thought you were saving.

Agents earn their income through commissions, but some may also charge transaction fees, which vary depending on the type of transaction. These fees are typically refundable at closing (or upon lease execution) to ensure transparency and avoid "double dipping."

From time to time, Buyers decide not to move forward or terminate a contract — often during the Due Diligence phase. Ironically, the better an Agent performs, the more likely they may end up not getting paid for their work. That's one reason there's a growing trend toward refundable transaction fees.

TRUST

People will give you the opportunity to earn their business if they like you — but they'll only do business with you if they trust you.

A real estate relationship is a lot like entering a joint venture — your Agent becomes your business partner (or your "work spouse"). Choose someone whose integrity, professionalism, and energy you genuinely believe in, because the right partnership makes all the difference in achieving your goals.

Expertise matters — especially when it comes to Due Diligence. Does your Agent truly understand all components of the transaction? If not, you could face serious financial consequences.

The REALTOR Code of Ethics, specifically Article 11, is clear: Agents must not engage in real estate activities or provide services outside their training or competency. Unfortunately, violations still happen — sometimes from good intentions, sometimes from overconfidence, and occasionally from greed.

Working with an experienced, well-trained professional isn't just a smart choice — it's your best protection.

Small Business Owners don't necessarily know what they are supposed to ask so my charge to you is – ask questions then ask questions about the answers they give you. Do you feel like you are an expert in this area of Commercial? Agents don't know everything but a good Agent knows they need to ask, and to whom. Also note, Agents can pay referral fees to referring Agents so if you are concerned about your favorite residential Agent not getting paid by going with someone else, just ask your Agent for help.

Sometimes having excellent critical thinking skills is more important than specific property skills. It all depends on the complexity of the transaction.

VALUE ADDED SERVICE

Agents are required to complete Mandatory Continuing Education (MCE) hours to renew licenses. Unfortunately, some treat it as a checkbox task — or turn it into a "MCE Cruise" that's more about fun than professional growth. There's nothing wrong with having fun, just not at the Client's expense.

Look for an Agent who's genuinely committed to learning and improving — someone who seeks to add value, not just collect MCE credits to meet minimum requirements or make "Alphabet Soup."

When you see letters after their name, ask what the designations are and how that benefits you.

In the commercial world, the most valuable designations include Certified Commercial Investment Member, Society of Industrial and Office Realtors, and Certified Commercial Sales Expert. But in my opinion, also having a business degree is a real value add!

QUICK REFERENCE TO SHOPPING FOR YOUR BROKER

- Licensing Regulations and Rules
- Agency
- Fiduciary
- Factors to Consider When Choosing your Broker

CHAPTER THREE

SHOPPING FOR PROPERTY FROM THE PROPERTY CENTRIC PERSPECTIVE

The chapter is specifically about the physical Property, not the qualitative Small Business Owner's needs. In terms of Feature-Benefit, it's the Feature.

END-USER TYPES FROM THE PROPERTY CENTRIC PERSPECTIVE

Commercial real estate use is generally categorized as Retail, Office, Industrial, Multifamily and Special Use. While you may have heard of Mixed-use or Live-Eat-Play, the use is a combination of these five.

Typically parcels have one zoning use, but in some cases, especially in gentrification areas, there may be multiple uses permitted (double entendre) on the one parcel. In some cases, like outside of city limits, (OCL), there typically is no zoning. However, a county (boroughs or parish) may have specific rules so it is important to always do your Due Diligence. If by chance you run into OCL in the parcel lookup, that does not necessarily mean that it is not zoned, it just means that the municipality may not have recorded it with the county or it is not updated. Again, like a broken record, do your Due Diligence.

Lastly on this note, your Agent should be aware of Extra Territorial Jurisdiction (ETJ). Cities plan their sprawl for decades in advance so they control its use as if they already have incorporated it. If it is ETJ or within a certain proximity to the city boundary, you need permits for development, even if just a partial tear down. They have the right to stop you, fine you, or force you to tear it down.

Speaking of, zoning, here's a quick look at some zoning from an End-User perspective. Since each municipality has their own zoning and there are ordinance overlays, is just an example from the City of San Antonio, but your city will be different. This is a sample but in reality, there are over two pages of zonings, without detailed explanations.

OFFICE

This use typically includes business service providers such as financial planners, insurance firms, accountants, consultants, therapists, attorneys, and real estate firms. That zoning code might look like O1, O2, and O3. The O obviously is for Office and the numbers indicate density, size, or such as it increases traffic and utility impact. The existing utilities and infrastructure must support the use. Density includes customer count, traffic impact, utilities and parking.

Office Users typically have similar needs and can readily utilize space from another Office User with little to no modification. For those reasons, it may be financially wise to buy a Multi-Tenant Office complex and become a Tenant of your investment. Consult your accountant for tax benefits.

MEDICAL OFFICE USERS

While technically speaking a Medical Office is an Office, there are some special considerations. The zoning for Medical is the same as Office for non-surgical use. For therapists, radiologists, family practices, and chiropractors, the standard Office zoning would be sufficient. However, some Medical may need hospital services so a H overlay would be required if they were going to build one. If you are going to build and want an H overlay, the Due Diligence is very important.

Two special considerations are surgery and illness when it comes to leasing to a medical practitioner in a standard Office complex or Multi-Tenant building. First, Medical and General Office don't mix well. Accountants and Attorneys who invite clients to their office for business are not exactly keen on exposing them to people bleeding, have runny noses or coughing, or worse. As a landlord it is important to plan your tenant mix. As an End User, it might give you some insight as to whether or not you want to lease in a building. Knowing the tenant mix is important. Second, Medical users have similar needs, such as surgical, lab work, and waiting area and typically go into medical office parks.

RETAIL USERS

Retail is as variable due to the number of consumer goods and services that exist. Retail may also include tax preparers, insurance companies, and loan officers, besides the typical nail salon, café, book store or liquor store. They all benefit by foot traffic. Tenant mix is important to assess the added value you may get from this, or not. Restaurants are also a Retail Use but sometimes are free standing like you see in larger restaurants like Olive Garden or Cheddars. The zoning for Retail could be C1, C2, or C3 (Commercial use) where C3 has the most flexibility for higher density or possible chemicals such as Auto Zone or Batteries Plus, which could have a chemical off gassing or liquid negative impact. I already mentioned special considerations with Medical so now I'll explain special considerations with Restaurants.

RESTAURANT USERS

Restaurants do make money from food sales of course, but they make a higher margin on alcohol sales, which requires a liquor license. Keep in mind that there may be ordinances and overlay districts that may restrict this. For example, it is not uncommon to have an ordinance for noise if too near residential, or alcohol if near a public school.

The zoning may not include such information, nor might the Landlord tell you; it's not his duty. Being that alcohol is a high profit item for

Restaurants and grease traps are required to operate, it might be prudent to perform Due Diligence before leasing or buying.

INDUSTRIAL USERS

Industrial is growing with the new focus on Built in America. In fact, just in the last few months I have come across many new developments geared toward logistics. Too, the growth of Amazon has grown warehousing. Typically, institutional Investors or large construction related businesses need this. Occasionally a local business like yourself might need it. HVAC companies might buy supplies in bulk, or perhaps there is a need for storing vehicles, vans, or other trucks. Auto repair business may also fall into this category as they have heavy oil and chemical.

It may be too that a Small Business Owner or Investor like yourself might want to participate in gentrification. I drive by this Industrial Park in an old part of town, just off the railroad, that took a large, outdated warehouse/distribution center with a large parking lot, which they converted into a hip, adult playground for sportsters. Besides the sports and Pickle Ball court, they have a restaurant and bar inside. They market it for sports but also host special events. Way cool!

Light Industrial is a little different, you would typically find that use in a C3 but could also fit into traditional Industrial too. These would commonly be found in Industrial Parks outside or at the edge of town. In San Antonio, TX we have the I-35 corridor that runs to Dallas/Ft Worth, but the San Antonio to Austin corridor is heavily used by businesses that service the two cities. It is about an hour to get from one to the other, but also many other mid towns have grown too. Thus, it would make good business sense to include restaurants, shops and breweries there too. So, they do.

Typically, Light Industrial falls into C3 zoning, including micro-breweries, automotive repair and servicing, and some textile industries. Special attention is required for environmental concerns.

The more hazardous, the more likely it will be Industrial zoning (I1, I2, I3, I4).

MIXED-USE USERS

This is my favorite category for many reasons, even though it's not really its own; It's a hybrid. I have a preference for C3 since almost any business can operate here except Heavy Industrial. Mixed-use is a combination of C3 & Residential, and sometimes Light Industrial. The San Antonio – Austin 35 corridor and the gentrification areas are Mixed-use. Another good example is the Pearl Brewery area and hopefully one day soon, the Lonestar Brewery facility will be re-developed. Both of these are former breweries dating back to 1883, when they brewed and used the San Antonio River to chill the beer.

QUICK REFERNCE TO SHOPPING FOR YOUR PROPERTY FROM THE PROPERTY CENTRICL PERSPECTIVE

- Property Centric Model
- End-User Types

CHAPTER FOUR

SHOPPING FOR PROPERTY FROM THE END-USER CENTRIC PERSPECTIVE

This chapter is about viewing real estate from an alternative perspective. Most people focus solely on the property itself — the location, the building, and the price. But I want you to think differently.

Your property shouldn't just be a line-item expense — it should be a functional business asset that actively drives success.

In other words, let your real estate work for you. Treat it as a sales force for your business, driving growth, visibility, and opportunity rather than simply occupying space.

I'm passionate about helping Small Business Owners thrive, and that starts with understanding how to make your property a strategic part of your business — not just a place where your business happens to be.

THE END-USER CENTRIC MODEL

I created this model to help you focus on real estate from a user perspective, or the benefit of the property rather than its features. Let's look at the principles marketing as it relates to real estate which I call, the 5 Ps of Real Estate.

Marketing 101 says to start with the 4 P's; I am saying 5 because your property is also a marketing tool. It's a simple concept but a powerful analysis tool.

PRODUCT

Your business is a product, whether it's a good or service. Your property is a reflection of your business, including its aesthetics, style, location, layout, convenience, parking, features, and design. The first impression effects how your customers or clients judge your business. If you don't think it matters that much, think about how you choose your restaurants, gas station, shopping center, and so on. How did the location, aesthetics, and building itself affect your opinion of the business and why you chose it?

PRICE

There is a value continuum that ranges from discount to luxury. Think about where your business fits into the continuum. A cheap property will give a cheap impression and a premium property will give a premium impression. What message do you want to convey? The appearance, price and location will determine your product's value (branding). Does your property support yours?

PROMOTION

How will you communicate that value to the market place? Are you wholesale or retail? Do you have walk-in traffic or are you a destination business? Are you advertising on media or are you selectively sending sophisticated special event announcements? Your property will act a promotions conduit. If you are a back-office operation then no visibility is just fine. But if you are an accounting or finance firm you need to be in a property that communicates your success.

PLACEMENT

As a Small Business Owner your emphasis should be on demographics, visibility, and accessibility. You can be in the most visible of places but if the surrounding area does not include your target market, the location may not be a good fit. Similarly, if the demographics support your business but your business is difficult to find, or the parking is difficult, then it may not be good location. One of the most challenging issues for most businesses today is the location and volatile market conditions. Sometimes it's better to lease than buy to manage cash flow or perhaps to build if you can ride on the coat tails of a nearby high-end center. The worst thing you can do is choose a bad location or mismatch demographics.

PROPERTY

Your business plan should include the right property and all of its benefits to promote the business effectively to get the best results.

Now that you can see how the 5Ps play into your decision, let's talk about a few strategic factors that move your property from the liability column to the asset column.

FEATURE-BENEFIT ANALYSIS

Think of your property from a benefit perspective rather than a feature perspective. A feature/benefit statement looks like this:

Feature/benefit Example 1

Feature statement: 4.23 acre lot for sale, behind the restaurant also for sale.

Benefit statement: Now offering 4.23 acre lot for a double drive though lane or more parking for customer convenience to the restaurant that is also for sale.

Suppose that you have a dry cleaning business. The option for a double drive-thru lane is strategic. This property should be viewed by a benefit value, to your customers and to your business model.

Feature/Benefit Example 2:

Feature statement: Highway frontage with great visibility and multiple ways for egress/ingress.

Benefit statement: Being on a highway frontage makes it easier for customers to create more walk-in business and the multiple ways to get in and out are convenient to the customers.

Suppose you have a minor emergency clinic. Avoiding additional stress during an already difficult situation and prevents them from going to a clinic with easier access is strategic.

Feature/Benefit Example 3:

Feature statement: A new high-profile Power Center.

Benefit statement: High foot traffic, visibility, and highway frontage with great demographics for greater sales revenue.

Based on a true story, a restaurant that originated out in Austin, TX, our sister city decided to open up their first location in San Antonio, TX. The restaurant failed to consider the impact of egress/ingress issue. The restaurant closed in less than six months. There was no immediate access into the actual restaurant space causing customers to drive down an extra block, U-turn, and pass several other restaurants before accessing their parking lot. The inconvenience and distractions were horrible.

SUSTAINABLE COMPETITIVE ADVANTAGE

Longaberger Baskets was a boutique company based out of Frazeysburg, OH. Although now closed, they hit the nail on the head with a statement about their business. Dave Longaberger, the founder, had a unique vision. His brand is valued for its quality and commitment to a common product – baskets. Their uncompromising commitment to quality and brand has kept them in the basket industry for 42 years. They closed in 2018 with a history that goes back to 1896.

Why are we talking about baskets? As much as your product is the key to your success, so is your property. Longaberger understood that which is why they branded their headquarters. They had a vision and cemented it literally as part of their business strategy.

TARGET MARKET

Your property reflects your value proposition and will resonate with your Target Market. You might not want to build a basket building, but it would be strategic to match your property with your product value, company mission statement, corporate culture, and your customer base.

Think about Buccees who builds ginormous gas stations in high traffic tourist locations and uses their oh-so-darn-cute beaver, Buccee, to pull us in to buy $50 of gas and $400 in snacks and dog clothes (with Buccee on it). McDonald's benefits being in Walmart stores, befitting their value system. You typically will see Class A high rise luxury office buildings clustered around each other and the hotels or spas will be similar. Other places that are even more posh, like the Disney Aulani Resort on Oahu, have rates starting at $2,000 for a 1-night stay in a 1-Bedroom Villa on in the off season, so they are surrounded by luxury retailers. Be cognizant of the location. If you are looking for luxurious clientele you may not want to build by a discount store.

To the restaurant restroom point I made earlier, I am sure that you have seen a property that has caused you to question a business' products (or service) by their appearance, location, convenience, parking, features, and design. A property can be the allure or deterrent. This value is based on what your customer (Target Market) thinks, not what I or anyone else thinks.

I'm a Texas girl, I love BBQ! I enjoy taking clients and out of town friends and family to Rudy's Country Store. Every Rudy's location is a barn, equipped with wood picnic tables, plain paper towel rolls, and a beverage trough. I hand my guests a plastic food tray to carry out their food then watch their face as they get their food. It's served on butcher paper and the sides are in cheap paper trays. Enhancing the experience, the server tears a loaf of bread in half with his hands, with the bag still intact, and plops it on the tray. It's quite entertaining to watch and it requires some talent to rip that bag as easily as they do. Their buildings clearly set the tone; they try to be in old gas stations or a country saloon, when possible, otherwise they build barns.

The guest asks about plates. What plates? There are no plates! The building is simple – a plain red barn, with unpainted tables, and a roll of paper towels. It matches their food perfectly, and that's what you need to do to maximize value. What traits of your business culture or product can be infused into your property?

DEMOGRAPHIC TRENDS

The Millennials continue to drive our market and now Gen Z! They grew up with a cell phone in their hand so it's an extension of their existence. My kids are Millennials so I understand. I always try to embrace change. Nothing ever stays the same so adapt or die, that is my philosophy on change.

I also always look for opportunity, which in this case is how to use ai, apps, and social media. Some current trends are mobile services like delivery services, package lockers (porch pirate prevention), app ordering for restaurants, and now virtual medial services. Millennials and Zs love these! How will you factor this into your business model? Don't become a Block Buster! They made the mistake thinking they were in the video business. They were in the entertainment business.

You need to evaluate how trends like this affect your business and know what your industry really is.

AGILITY

Politics, economics, and technology also drive trends. Look at the Covid impact. We have plan for the unexpected. A mediterranean café that I used to frequent closed during Covid and was replaced with Cava Digital Kitchen. I found it interesting that while this was happening, and I was stuck at home like most of us were, I was watching Chef David Chang talk about what's next for restaurants post Covid. But it was already happening. Cava Digital Kitchen set up an app based ordering system with drive-thru and curbside service. They only have a few tables or dine in, and small, not for parties at all. This is being agile and future thinking.

Every 7 years there is a tech shift. Sometimes the change is un-noticeable until it bites you in the butt. In other cases, it can be like the streaming revolution that blindsided Blockbuster. Follow the "Twenty Something's" – they will always be the trend. It doesn't mean to ignore your core, shoot, Cracker Barrell learned that fast and furious! You need to know how to be inclusive without being exclusive.

One of my favorite reads is Spencer Johnson's "Who Moved My Cheese." Do you see the writing on the wall? Don't build your life around the cheese so hard that when it moves you can't. It's chalked full of thinking modification analogies.

The dining industry is a good example of a current real estate trend. Restaurant owners with expensive leases complain that it's not fair that food trucks can set up the way they do without the overhead.

LIFE RULE #1 *Life isn't fair.*

LIFE RULE #2*, Look for the cheese. A good hockey player plays where the puck is. A great hockey player plays where the puck is going to be. – Wayne Gretskey*

Small Business Owners need to think strategically, all encompassing, which means to use your property to grow your business and plan for the unexpected. To be successful you need to plan for the future and be agile enough to make changes, to adapt. Are you good or great?

QUICK REFERENCE TO SHOPPPING FOR YOUR PROPERTY FROM THE END-USER CENTRIC PERSPECTIVE

- End-User Centric Model
- 5 Ps of Real Estate
- Feature-Benefit Analysis
- Sustainable Competitive Advantage

CHAPTER FIVE

FINANCIAL WISE

On the first day of class, I told my M.B.A. Finance Professor, Prof. Kadapakkam that numbers were not my strong suit. I requested that he not call on me in class. I promised, in return, that I would always do my homework and would show it to him before each class.

Prof. K responded, "May I ask what is your concentration?" I answered, "Marketing Strategy." Prof. K. said, "Don't you think that in Marketing you have to deal with budgets?" To which I politely replied, "Well of course, but I'm interested in Consumer Behavior not budgets." Prof. K said, "Quite frankly I'm not really sure why you are getting an M.B.A. if you don't want to master Managerial Finance. Cathy, money is the core of business, and if you don't want to know how to measure profitability then perhaps you shouldn't get an M.B.A." Wow! That hit me pretty hard. From that day forward Prof. K called on me every single class.

Later that semester he asked the class a question about a case study. I thought I knew the answer but was afraid to say it out loud; I saw a Marketing answer. I didn't want 60 students laughing at me though, if I was wrong. Like scared deer, nobody was answering; he called on us one at a time, and shot down one student after another until he gazed over at me. "Cathy, I know you know the answer, why aren't you raising your hand?" Inside my head I was thinking *Could it be as simple as a Marketing answer?* I said it – "To be a sustainable in business you need to have a Sustainable Competitive Advantage."

The class waited in suspense to hear his response, with a little snickering here and there. Prof. K, with great joy said, "*It doesn't matter what price you charge or how many glasses of lemonade that you sell, if you don't have a Sustainable Competitive Advantage eventually the business will fail."*

The Finance students grumbled saying this is a Finance Class not Marketing. Prof. K said, "This young lady was brave enough to take my Managerial Finance Class and has done her homework every day. How many of you are doing your homework diligently? Business is a system. It works together with other departments. Without Marketing, we wouldn't have anything to measure. That was the highlight of my semester and the beginning of my true appreciation for Managerial Finance, and Prof. K.

To better understand the financial lending, I will cover the benefit of being prepared before shopping for your property.

NEGOTIATION POSITION

Preparing financially means that you put yourself in the best negotiation position possible. If multiple offers being considered for the same property the Landlord/Seller will choose the most verifiably financially sound, safest option, even if the lesser is willing to pay more. Your Agent's job is to get you to the first position, which means you need to get your financials in order.

If you are going to lease, you are offering a cash flow to the Landlord so that he can pay the mortgage, expenses, and receive a return on investment. They are going to do everything possible to ensure you are the right Tenant, adding value to the center, and improving foot traffic to the other Tenants in the center so everyone maximizes profitability opportunity.

TIP: *If you feel that you don't quite have the necessary funds, you should take good notes from Chapter 5 Financial Wise. There are plenty of creative resources.*

BUDGETING

I highly recommend that you use accounting software or an accountant to properly measure your cash flow and business health. Not only should you do your monthly books, you should run profit and loss statements monthly, and compare year over year.

It is also important to create budgets. The profit and loss measures actuals, but budgeting and forecasting helps your business. Set goas. Set KPIs (Key Performance Indicators). Create a monthly budget with a quarterly review to check your actuals against your forecasted, personally and professionally. Think one, three, five and maybe years into the future. Figure out your capital access and cash flow. A good Agent will be able to help you with lenders and creative capital access. You need to have consistent and detailed records.

Once you have an idea of how much you can afford then you are ready to share this information with your Agent. If your intentions are to purchase, then you are ready to meet with the lender.

COMMERCIAL LOANS

Types of commercial real estate loans include Permanent Financing for long-term ownership, Bridge Loans for short-term needs while waiting for permanent financing, Construction Loans for development projects, and SBA Loans backed by the Small Business Administration for favorable terms. Other options are Hard Money Loans for fast-paced projects, CMBS Loans (Commercial Mortgage-Backed Securities) sold to Investors, and Mezzanine Financing for additional capital beyond a traditional mortgage.

LONG-TERM & CONVENTIONAL LOANS

Permanent Financing: A long-term loan for acquiring or refinancing existing properties, used by Investors to purchase income-producing properties. These can come from banks, life insurance companies, or government-sponsored entities.

Conventional Commercial Mortgages: Similar to traditional residential mortgages but for businesses, requiring significant down payments and established business history.

SHORT-TERM LOANS

Bridge Loans: Short-term loans used to bridge a funding gap until a more permanent loan is secured, or to fund renovations to increase a property's value.

Hard Money Loans: Short-term loans with higher interest rates, typically offered by private lenders and used when speed is critical or traditional financing isn't an option.

DEVELOPMENT & ACQUISITION LOANS

Construction Loans: Provided to finance new construction projects from the ground up.

SBA Loans (7(a) and 504): Government-backed loans offering favorable terms, lower down payments, and longer repayment periods to small businesses.

USDA Business and Industry (B&I) Loans: Support rural development by providing financing for property improvement and economic growth in these areas.

OTHER FINANCING OPTIONS

CMBS Loans: Commercial Mortgage-Backed Securities, where loans are bundled and sold as bonds to Investors.

Mezzanine Financing: A hybrid debt-equity financing option that is subordinate to the primary mortgage but senior to equity.

Life Company Loans: Loans from life insurance companies, which often provide long-term, stable financing options for commercial properties.

Let's take a look at lender considerations and qualifying factors.

Small Business Owners may consider the SBA Loan but it must be owner occupied. That doesn't mean 100% used by the Owner but the business that seeks the loan must be using the property. The program has some merit but other options might be a better fit for you.

Choose a lender based on your specific needs, banking history, and financial status. You may want to shop rates, but there are other factors to consider such as customer service and ability to qualify such as flexible plans, better customer support, help with asset management, or perhaps you just feel like the relationship is a better fit. Don't only consider rates.

Private Lenders are a good choice if you don't think you'll conform to traditional lenders or need to move quickly assuming your business has consistent, solid cash flow. Most importantly, look for quality, responsive customer service since poor customer service can be a real Debbie Downer especially when it affects the transaction process. There are financial protection periods but if those deadlines are missed this can cause the business to default and lose the property and the earnest money. These loans are 100% asset based so credit scores and personal financials are not typically required, however, you will need to have substantial funds and proof thereof, and the asset has to make sense to the lender. Be prepared to answer a lot of questions about the property and your business, as well as bank statements for proof of funds.

Here's a quick overview of the Small Business Administration (SBA) Loan Program.

The SBA programs typically require 10% down or collateral or both, depending on the loan type and your financial status. If you don't have 20-30% (plus closing costs and inventory), but you have good credit and a solid business, the SBA may be a great option for you. There is also an option for a Microloan for a start-up up to $50,000.

SMALL BUSINESS LOANS (SBA)

SBA loans are small business loans provided by banks and other lenders that are partially guaranteed by the U.S. Small Business Administration (SBA). The SBA's guarantee reduces risk for lenders, allowing them to offer more favorable terms like longer repayment periods and lower down payments for small businesses. While the SBA doesn't directly lend money (except in disaster situations), they set the guidelines and provide the guarantee that makes these loans possible for businesses.

BENEFITS OF SBA LOANS

- Competitive terms
- Lower down payments
- Longer repayment term
- Flexible requirements

Consider Ms. Jennifer. A typical Small Business Owner, Jennifer doesn't like to pay income tax so she classifies some personal expenses as business expenses. Sometimes it's hard to say if their event is personal or business; I understand this dilemma; it happens. She buys a car in the firm's name, pays for an administrative assistant who might also run personal errands, puts all dining and entertainment on the business card but not all were work related. It can be bothersome and complicated especially when wearing so many business hats.

In this case, a gross income of $500,000 might actually look like $400,000 if $100,00 is incorrectly expensed. Because it is documented by IRS, if Jennifer put down $500,000 net income instead of $400,000 her loan would be denied. She could file an amended return to correct it but that might take a while and that would cause a tax payment that she may not have. Discuss with your CPA.

However, if she can demonstrate to a Private Capital Lender that she can re-arrange those finances for better cash flow, she may be a good candidate for a Private Capital Loan.

Another example is Bobby Jo, a veteran real estate investor who owns twenty houses with an asset value in the range of $2,000,000 in assets (no debt). She's 100% leased on all ten properties with a $20,000 monthly cash flow ($240,000 a year). Bobby Jo decides to exchange all her houses for a retail strip center listed for $5,000,000, which is also 100% leased. She needs to borrow $3,000,000. Bobby Jo's credit score is less than stellar, even though the deal terms are very good and she has a proven track record the bank rejects her because she doesn't fit the bank's business model.

Jennifer and Bobby Jo are perfect candidates for Private Capital Funds since non-fiduciary lenders have flexible requirements. They understand that some Businesses Owners may not be very good with their books.

OTHER FUNDING SOURCES

CREDIT CARDS – While the interest rates may be high, this could be a good short term solution like a bridge loan.

HELOC LOANS is a revolving line of credit that lets homeowners borrow against the **equity** in their home — similar to how a credit card works, but with your house as collateral.

SELLER/OWNER FINANCING - the seller acts as the lender.

RETIREMENT FUNDS like 401(k) for real estate investing – tap into your retirement funds to buy property — but do it carefully to avoid taxes and penalties. You generally can't **directly buy real estate** with a regular 401(k). But you can roll it over into a self-directed IRA (SDIRA), which allows investments in real estate, notes, or private placements. An **IRA for real estate investing** — specifically a **Self-Directed IRA (SDIRA)** — allows you to use retirement funds to buy and hold real estate assets, instead of just stocks or mutual funds. You should read up on this carefully especially regarding arm's length.

REAL ESTATE SYNDICATION is a way for multiple investors to pool money together to buy a property or portfolio that would be too expensive for one person alone — like apartment complexes, shopping centers, or office buildings. This is regulated by the Securities and Exchange Commission.

CROWD FUNDING is similar to Syndications but is amongst friends and family without the SEC filings and is for smaller amounts of money and is online.

QUICK REFERENCE TO FINANCIAL WISE

- Negotiation Position
- Budgeting
- Commercial Loans
- Small Business Loans
- Commercial Bank Requirements
- Private Capital Loans
- Other Funding Sources

CHAPTER SIX

LEASE VS. BUY AND WHY

Leasing is typically where most businesses start when it comes to brick and mortar to keep risk and costs down. In some cases, it I just necessary or there are other motives and deeper pockets, then there are more options. Lease new space or second generation, Build to Suit, Buy an existing building, or build. To make an informed decision you need to look at your big picture. Factors to consider besides required capital, includes:

OPPORTUNITY COST

Funds are always limited in some capacity. When you decide to spend money on one thing, that is money that you cannot spend on something else. If you spend $500,000 on a fleet of moving vans for your business, what did you give up to spend that money? Could you have leased the fleet and have spent that money on marketing or another business location? Did this deplete reserves?

In terms of real estate, if you are an air condition company and you lease your building, could you have money to lease a bigger fleet to do more air condition jobs? By spending that $500,000 on real estate then you would have less sales, possibly. Or did it make more sense to buy so you wouldn't potentially have to move upon lease expiration? These opportunity costs are part of the lease vs. buy decision.

GENERATIONAL WEALTH

Is your decision to buy to build generational wealth, or it is part of a bigger business plan and you have the financial and physical resources to see it through? If so, buy. If not, then it may be better to lease. Sometimes it is better to just keep your business as a lease and invest in something that can run itself like a Multifamily property.

TAX BENEFITS

There are pros and cons both ways. Owning your business location offers significant tax advantages, such as deducting the mortgage expense, property taxes, and depreciation, which can lower taxable income and still build equity over time. Leasing also provides tax benefits, as rent is deductible, but you miss out on the long-term wealth-building and tax opportunities of ownership. It would be prudent to do a detailed cash flow analysis considering tax rates, loan terms, and expected property appreciation is essential to determine the most beneficial option. Your accountant can help you with this.

AGILTY

Growth and relocation considerations are important especially in today's volatile economy. Last year eggs were gold. This year tariffs are bringing business back to the US. If you buy, you should include a strategy to compensate for market changes. You may want to grow in size, or by adding new locations. Or you may find that the plant that was supposed to open is taking much longer or doesn't. Leasing gives you more flexibility due to only being locked in for a short period of time and requires less capital. But there is still risk. You may sign a five-year lease and spend a lot of money on Tenant Improvements, but may not be able to renew, and you lose those improvements.

***TIP**: Write in renewal options. If they sell, write in a Right of First Refusal option.*

RISK MANAGEMENT

Let's be real for a moment, none of us has a Magic 8 Ball and cannot predict the future.

***LIFE RULE #3** Everything changes, often unexpected.*

***LIFE RULE #4:** We all expire.*

It is prudent to factor in risk management to thrive and use change to your advantage, and to survive. Some key factors include the market, government, and demographics.

Market (industry) or Demographic Changes - Who knew Covid was going to hit or even existed? While that is an extreme situation, there are unexpected situations like personal medical emergencies, a fire, etc. that may cause a temporary change or perhaps a permanent change that requires more money to facilitate. If it is tied up in a building then that could be problematic. Leasing might be better if there are liquidity issues because even if the business plan is great, you can't forecast the unexpected.

Government Changes –Change in administration or policies, city, state, federal or international, change may impact your business. What are some ways that you can prepare for that?

Opportunity Costs - What if the desired location, building or lot size, or layout is not available to buy? You will need to choose which is more important, buying in a different area, leasing, or another suitable option (a different building or size). What else could you do with that money? You could get a different location, more locations, or increase your marketing budget. Would you benefit by having a unique value proposition in the building that you buy or would one with more parking be better?

Exit Strategy – This is pretty self-explanatory and very unique to each Small Business Owner. I just wanted to spur your thinking because of certainty, Life Rules #3 and #4. Do you have an exit strategy? Do you have a succession plan? Do you have life insurance (whole or universal is smarter for investment reasons)? Do you plan to sell the business? These are all important considerations. You do not want to leave your business partners or your family in jeopardy.

OWNER OCCUPIED VS. NON-OWNER INVESTORS

Owner Occupied and Non-Owner Buyers (Investors) are as different as cats and dogs. The Owner Occupied will have End User needs and an emotional connection, unlike the Investor; sort of like residential vs. commercial buying. All the factors discussed are relevant to both, but the decision itself will be passion vs. ROI.

If you have been in business for at least three years, are liquid, and can afford to buy, build, or remodel what you want, and the opportunity is there, then most certainly do it. Sometimes it's a capital-intensive business, like Medical or Restaurant, again, that makes sense to buy or build; they also tend to stay put. I also think it's wise to buy a Multi-Tenant property and lease out the other space for the same reason Kiyosaki likes Multifamily. Most everyone needs a place to do business and leasing is more common, easier, less capital is needed, and less time commitment.

Are You Mentally Ready?

It's a big deal to bite off an investment that is illiquid. Being a Small Business Owner in and of itself creates considerable strains on one's personal life, so adding real estate will create even more demand on time and money. Be prepared to do it right.

Are You Financially Ready?

Your personal finances must be in order. Regardless of leasing, buying or building, you will need to be prepared to build-out, for maintenance, and repairs, both in terms of time and money, and evaluate how it will impact your personal world. Your family should be on board too. It may delay or prevent some personal purchases or needs.

Are You Physically Ready?

Just like for your personal residence you have lawn care, trash care, house maintenance, house cleaning, and so forth. Unless you have a good investor behind you or a line of credit, you may find yourself scrubbing toilets on occasion or your kids might be folding some napkins. It happens. It can be long hours. It can be intensive.

Are You Ready to Invest?

Investing means to create wealth though cash flows and asset growth; get off the rat race wheel. A Robert Kiyosaki principal is to leverage money, also known as Other People's Money (OPM). Only take on debt that can be cash flowed by the entity which is leveraged.

Kiyosaki advocates investing in Multifamily properties and living in it, such that the leased units pay for the mortgage resulting in free living for the owner. This principle applies to business too; Multi-Tenant is less risk. If you really want to live in a single-family home then find another investment that yields enough cash flow to pay for your mortgage, resulting in living free.

OPM is leveraging your assets, and can be a good debt. Invest in a Multi-Tenant Commercial space, lease it back to your business, and collect income from yourself (tax benefit) and the other Tenants.

Small Business Owners need to understand the WHY behind the BUY before choosing buying or leasing. Once you do, and are prepared, buying is a very smart decision for tax savings, cash flow, retirement and generational wealth.

The following questions are designed to help you critically evaluate leasing vs. buying. This decision is unique to you so you should develop a customized pros and cons list after reviewing these questions then prepare a strategy upon completing the book. Even better, write notes in the blank pages to keep organized.

KEY QUESTIONS BEFORE LEASING OR BUYING PROPERTY

- What are your primary business goals?
- What is your core business focus, and how does this property support it?

- How will this investment impact daily operations and long-term growth?
- Have you maintained financial stability for at least three years?
- How much capital is required for build-out, maintenance, and ongoing expenses?
- What are the current and emerging trends in your industry and market?
- How adaptable is your business to changing market conditions?
- What level of financial risk are you comfortable with?
- How much control over the property do you want/need?
- What are the opportunities?
- What are the costs if you lease vs. buy?
- Would your business better benefit one way or the other?
- Will the property provide added value to your business as a lease vs. buy?
- Can you realistically afford to lease or buy given your current and projected financials?
- Do you need/want the tax benefits that ownership may offer?

QUICK REFERENCE TO LEASE VS. BUY

- Equity Opportunity
- Generational Wealth
- Tax Benefits
- Agility
- Risk Management
- Key Questions Before Leasing or Buying Property

CHAPTER SEVEN

NEGOTIATIONS

Some people hate negotiating as much or more than public speaking, but as a Certified Negotiation Expert (CNE) and my competitive nature, I like it.

People dynamics are interesting; understanding what people want and how to satisfy everyone to the extent they are willing to sign an agreement fascinates me. It's like sitting on a bench at Six Flags in front of The Rattler when somebody in a group decides they don't want to get on the ride. There's a lot of negotiating and concessions in that deal.

In the second part of this chapter, I'll introduce you to basic leasing and purchasing contracts. One thing you should know about contracts is that they both require certain clauses, so once you've become familiar with a leasing or purchase contract, it gets easier. For now, let's look at 5 strategic tips I'd like to share with you.

5 STRATEGIC NEGOTIATION TIPS

1. **Be Financially Prepared**
   Financial planning has already been discussed in depth but I cannot stress enough its critical role, especially in negotiations. If two offers are submitted for the same property the Landlord/Seller will choose the most verifiably, financially sound, Buyer/Tenant, even if the other is willing to pay more.

   Financial readiness demonstrates that you are prepared to go through the deal with minimal hiccups.

2. **Be Creative**
   There's usually more than one way to achieve an outcome. I had a client that needed to accommodate 20-30 new sales people but she didn't have the immediate funds for the office. She bought an existing business and still needed to train these people and buy office furniture, etc. Within 12 months she could afford the bigger space and within 24 months she could be very profitable.

   Thinking smartly, I proposed a payment structure to the Landlord that aligned with the Tenant's future cash flows that yielded the same average financial benefit to the Landlord over the term of the lease, just structured lower up front. Additionally, I negotiated six months of Rent Abatement (free rent) in exchange for a longer term, and took the space as-is. To make it even more lucrative to the Landlord, the Tenant paid a double deposit. It was a win-win.

3. **Be Flexible**
   Tenants always want to minimize their cash outlay on Tenant Improvements in leasing transactions, and deferred maintenance on sales. Look for ways to be flexible and cooperative in the negotiation. Look for the common objectives.

   On another transaction where only paint and carpet were offered, I negotiated additional Tenant Improvements. They wanted new paint, urban carpet squares, and a beautiful front door. That was all within budget until they added a request for specialty floors and lights. I worked out an arrangement with a flooring company that was willing to sell the product at a discount to get the deal done. The client did without the lights to stay within budget but had the right to change them at their expense when they could afford it.

   LIFE RULE #5*: You can't always get what you want. But if you try sometimes, well, you might find, you get what you need."- Rolling Stones*

4. **Understand Basic Real Estate Terminology**
   I've included Leasing Basics, Buying and Building, and my S.M.A.R.T. Decision Planner. Understanding this will be quite useful to understand what is negotiable. Depending on the value you give to the Landlord, and how experienced you are at negotiations, most terms are negotiable.

5. **Know what you can live with and without**
   An experienced negotiator who knows how to play in high stakes situations understands that the Rolling Stones are right.

   Keep in mind that you need to keep these crucial conversations respectful. Once you offend or annoy the other party, it is hard to come back from there and sometimes can kill the deal. As an experienced negotiator I will say that the optional outcome to any negotiation is that each party's core needs need to be met and each party feels like they've given up something they'd rather not; experiencing a little pain.

   Know your limits ahead of time, build in an exit strategy, and be willing to walk away if you can't get what you need; the proverbial line in the sand. If you have watched or know how Donald Trump negotiates, he always has a line and he is willing and does at time walk away. That is a hard but is a powerful tool.

With these strategic tips in mind, let's look at negotiation styles.

NEGOTIATION STYLES

Competitive Win-Lose Hard Bargaining vs. Collaborative Win-Win Negotiating

Harvard University has this to say about Competitive Win-Lose Hard Bargaining Negotiating.

"Competitive style negotiators pursue their own needs - yes, even when this means others suffer. They usually don't want to cause others to suffer and lose; they are just so narrowly focused on their shorter-term gains that they plunder obliviously through negotiations like a pirate. They often use whatever power and tactics they can muster, including their personality, position, economic threats, brand strength or size or market share. At its extreme negotiators call their behavior aggressive or psychotic."

Most people confuse "Win-Win" or the collaboration style with the compromising style. This is most definitely not the case. "Win-Win" is about making sure both parties have their needs met, and as much mutual value as can be created is created. A good Win-Win approach involves the following:

Core Principles of Harvard's Win-Win (Principled) Negotiation

- **Separate the People from the Problem**
- **Don't let emotions, egos, or personal attacks derail.**
  - Build trust and maintain relationships while addressing the substantive issues.
- **Focus on Interests, Not Positions**
- **Positions = what each side says they want (e.g., "I need $1M for this property").**
- **Interests = the underlying motivations, needs, or fears** driving those positions (e.g., "I need financial security" or "I want long-term tenants").
  - By uncovering interests, you find room for creative solutions.

- **Invent Options for Mutual Gain**
    - Brainstorm multiple possibilities before deciding.
    - Look for trade-offs—one side may value something the other finds less costly to give.
    - Think "expand the pie" instead of fighting over fixed slices.
- **Insist on Using Objective Criteria**
    - Base agreements on fair standards: market value, industry benchmarks, expert opinions, legal precedent.
    - This removes arbitrariness and strengthens legitimacy.

Tragically, too many people are overly accommodating and compromising, resulting in competitive style negotiators (Buyers/ Sellers/Landlords/Tenants) claiming more than their fair share. When these same competitive style buyers come up against skilled collaborative style negotiators, the competitive styles blunt coercion methods don't get rewarded with concessions. Negotiators are stretched and under tremendous time pressure, so there is temptation to compromise rather than time invested in collaborating wins out.

Negotiating contracts is important, and the one with the best strategies and knows their contracts well, will achieve the best results. It also helps with personal relationships.

QUICK REFERENCE TO NEGOTIATING

- 5 Strategic Negotiation Tips
- Negotiation Styles

CHAPTER EIGHT

COMMERCIAL REAL ESTATE CONTRACTS

I have to put out the standard real estate disclaimer that I am not an attorney and you should seek the advice of a licensed attorney.

Commonly I say "Agreement" in lieu of "Contract" but they are the same; I prefer "Agreement" to communicate the integral meaning. It isn't just something to sign, it is something that both parties ultimately must agree upon. I like "The Law Handbook" explanation of the basic elements of a contract:

A contract is much more than an agreement between two people. There must be an offer and acceptance, intention to create a legally binding agreement, a price paid (not necessarily money), a legal capacity to enter a contract of your own free will, and proper understanding and consent of what is involved. Any duress, false statements, undue influence or unconscionable dealings could make a contract illegal and void.

These required elements include:

- Offer and acceptance
- Intention to create legal relations
- Consideration
- Legal capacity
- Consent
- Illegal and void contracts

In some states, all agreements must be in writing. This means, something written on a sticky note may hold up better in court than a he/said she/said (even with a witness). Today, electronic communication constitutes as "in writing" including emails communications, email acknowledgements, e-signatures, and text messaging. Always be mindful of what you communicate electronically, especially bcc and forwarding.

COMMERCIAL REAL ESTATE PURCHASE/SALES CONTRACTS

Buying and Leasing start in the same way, using similar decision criteria. But they differ with regard to Due Diligence and financing. If you have bought a house, hopefully with a knowledgeable Agent, you are familiar already. Once the decision has been made to pursue a particular property, the next phase is to negotiate the contract.

Purchase/Sale contracts can be as brief as 20 pages or as complex as 45-60 pages. Attorneys have libraries through their bar association. For some reason, their contracts tend to be at least 20% more pages than the ones that come from a real estate library such as your state's real estate commission or Texas Association of Realtors (TAR) library. There are pros and cons for both, but certainly I prefer the ones from the Texas Real Estate Commission or TAR as they are generally fair to both sides and easier for non-attorneys to understand due to the standardized language throughout their library and familiarity.

The process by which we enter into the Purchase/Sales Contract is listed here. This checklist outlines the key steps in a typical commercial real estate purchase. Use it as a guide to track progress and meet deadlines. No two transactions are the same and definitely the type of sale will create various timelines and criteria. This is a general guideline.

COMMERCIAL REAL ESTATE PURCHASE CHECKLIST

- ❑ **Pre-Acquisition Planning:** Define investment goals. Assemble the team (broker, attorney, lender, accountant, inspector, etc.). Get financing pre-qualified.

- ❑ **Establish entity structure (LLC/partnership)**. Establish your bank account. Track this well; banks prefer seasoned capital but if it isn't then documenting its sources i.e. letters from Investors and their identity, especially if foreign. Your identification and Employer Identification Number (EI) will be required so get it done early if it is a new account.

- ❑ **Property Search & Initial Evaluation:** Identify target properties. Preliminary underwriting. Tour the property.

- ❑ **Letter of Intent (LOI):** Non-binding agreement outlining price, Due Diligence, earnest money, financing, and closing.

- ❑ **Purchase & Sale Agreement:** Legally binding contract with contingencies, warranties, remedies, and terms.

- ❑ **Due Diligence Period:** Review Title commitment, financial review (rent rolls, expenses, taxes). Legal review (title, zoning, survey, environmental). Physical inspections (roof, HVAC, structural). Market analysis. Secure financing. This could be days, weeks, or months subject to the type of property and business.

- ❑ **Financing & Appraisal:** Loan application & underwriting. Appraisal ordered and reviewed. Loan commitment issued.

- ❑ **Closing Preparation:** Finalize title & escrow. Review closing statement. Wire your funds.
- ❑ **Closing:** Sign documents (deed, loan, transfer). Transfer funds. Transfer title.
- ❑ **Take possession and enjoy!**

For more details about contracts speak with a local Real Estate Attorney or Licensed Real Estate Broker since this varies by state.

Up to now the Purchase/Sales Contract has been the topic, but let's talk about Lease Agreements next.

I find that most people understand or are familiar with purchasing and the terminology because they have typically purchased a home. Except for a few items, the contract terminology is generally the same. Leasing however, is very different.

To understand Leasing, it would be good to be familiar with basic terminology and what can be negotiated. You do not need to be an expert, that is why you hire an Agent, but to be familiar with these terms will help you toward your objective.

BASIC LEASING TERMS

- **Letter of Intent (LOI) sometimes just called a proposal** – Non binding agreement on negotiable items.
- **Execution Date** – The date on which all required signatures and initials are finalized. At this point, the lease becomes binding, and while typically there are no further changes, it may possibly be amended.

- **Occupancy Date** – The date the tenant officially takes possession of the premises, typically coinciding with move-in.
- **Expiration Date** – The date the lease term ends. If the tenant remains in the space beyond this date without a renewal, it is considered a "Holdover" tenancy, which often carries significant financial penalties (commonly a per diem rate many times higher than the base rent).
- **Lease Renewal** – If the tenant has an option to renew the lease, the specific terms and conditions will be detailed in this clause.
- **Base Rate** – The rental rate for the space, usually quoted per square foot on an annual basis.
- **Escalations** – Scheduled rent increases applied over the lease term, typically expressed as a percentage or fixed amount.
- **Options** – Additional rights that may be negotiated into the lease, such as renewal, early termination, relocation rights, or the right of first refusal on adjacent or available space.
- **Usable Square Feet (USF)** – The portion of the premises dedicated solely to the tenant's use, measured according to BOMA standards (Building Owners and Managers Association).
- **Rentable Square Feet (RSF)** – The tenant's USF plus a proportionate share of the building's common areas (such as lobbies, corridors, restrooms, elevators, and break rooms).
- **Pro-Rata Share** – The actual amount of the applied percentage of the building's common areas allocated to the tenant, added to their USF to calculate the RSF.

- **Add-On Factor (Load Factor)** – The percentage of common space that will be added to the usable square footage, representing the building's efficiency.

LEASE STRUCTURES AND EXPENSES

In the first edition I went way too far into lease structures. I have a tendency to want to spell out everything, as you may have already noticed. This time I put this section through the WIFFM lens; What's In It for Me? I will only cover the most common options. I will also explain some different types property classes and rate structures to help you understand how Agent's price properties and for Small Business Owners to make prudent decisions.

BASE RATE STRUCTURES

The most common Base Rate Structure is a Step Lease except for retail, which you are possibly going to see a Percentage Lease.

Step Lease, just like it sounds, the rate step increases annually to account for inflation. It would be a base rate for year one and a slight increase each year through the end of the term such as $24.00, $25.00, $26.00, $27.00 & year 5 ends with $28.00.

The Percentage Lease creates an incentive to the Landlord to value engineer the shopping center to increase sales revenues for the Tenants. The Property Management (PM) sometimes hosts events to bring in more foot traffic. It also incentivizes the PM to keep the center fully leased with desirable Tenants.

This type includes base rate plus a percentage of their sales. For example, a 3,000 sf space @ $10.00 sf per year ($0.8334 per mo.) would be $2,500 per mo. If sales were $200,000 that month then it would be $2,500 + $ 6,000 = $8,500 total for the month.

Those are Base Rate Structures, but then there are still shared property expenses to maintain the building and parking lots.

What expenses you might ask? Property expenses specific to the property that are not income to the Landlord, aka Pass through expenses. While you will still need to carry property insurance and pay your personal property taxes on furniture, fixtures, and equipment, the property expenses are passed on to the Tenant.

I promised not to get to in depth on the leasing so I am keeping it simple. Your Agent can get into the specifics.

Net Leases – Base rent is Net of Property Insurance, Taxes, and Common Area Maintenance (CAMs) that are allocated to Tenants as a percentage of their USF.

CAMs are parking lot maintenance, landscaping, dumpsters, etc.

In Office leasing, sometimes they are rolled in since they are consistent – Office users generally use the same amount of utilities, property insurance, etc. and they are given a set number of parking spaces. This is known as a **Full-Service Gross lease.**

The bottom line is, you need a good Agent to help you understand your options and know what can and cannot be negotiated.

DOLLARS AND SENSE

Now that you know the basic terms, let's talk about how they play into your decision making.

Let's say that you are considering 2 properties that we shall call A & B. Assume everything is the same i.e. location, and property size/layout. Each have different value propositions, though.

- **Property A: 10,000 sf at $24 FSG Year 1**
  - 18% Add-On Factor
  - Complimentary large, well-appointed conference room
  - large food court with dining on the main level
  - complimentary gym

- **Property B: 10,000 sf at $21 FSG Year 1**
  - 9% Add-On Factor
  - small café walk-up and take out. No seating.

Property A is be $20,000/mo. Property B is be $17,500/mo.

B is more economical at first glance as you'd save $2,500 a month over A. But what about the add on factor and amenities?

Property A 10,000 RSF at 18% would be 8,800 USF. Property B 10,000 RSF would be 9,100 USF. The difference in usable would be 800 square feet. If the spaces yield the same number of offices, etc. it seems like the difference of usable is not too relevant on space. However, it might yield a storage room for confidential files or a pod cast room. Property A has a large, free, shared conference room that would mean that you don't need that in-suite conference room, which could be another office. Also, that gym might draw healthier employees with less sick days and higher productivity from that extra energy, for better work efficiency and happier employees for employee retention and better recruiting. The dining hall could save some time and stress also resulting in happier, healthier people. So now, is that $2,500 a month a negative or a positive to your business?

These real-life scenarios exist. One way to navigate these options is to know your corporate culture. Do you want to encourage wellness? Do you want to have company events on site? Do you want a pod cast room? My point is that it is important to think beyond dollars and cents because sometimes more dollars make more sense.

PROPERTY CLASSIFICTIONS

We have gone over classifications of properties but not so much about specifics that might dictate why one office building might be $44.00 sf and another $32.00 sf and still another $14.00 sf. It would be helpful to be aware of how properties are classified.

OFFICE

Class A, B, or C defines the age, condition, and amenities of a property. I like analogies so think of hotel stars. Class A is a 5 Star resort, which typically is a high-rise, newer, and amenities. Class B is more like a 4 Star hotel with one or two amenities and is older but updated. Class C is, well, Class C, a Budget Inn. It gets the job done in spite of the numerous deferred maintenance issues. If you are going to go this direction, have proper expectations. There is a reason the rent is cheap. A high rise, low rise can be A, B, or C but generally office parks or garden parks are B or C.

RETAIL

In Retail "Class" terms aren't usually used but it helps my clients understand the quality of the center. The types of centers include Power Center, Mall, Neighborhood Center, Strip Center, and Mixed-Use also referred to as Live, Eat, Play. Mostly the End User is more concerned with the anchor, the traffic counts in the area, the demographics, clientele, parking, signage and cleanliness.

BUILD-TO-SUITS AND PAD SITES

Have you ever noticed when you are out shopping you see a stand-alone building that has its own exterior design? Appleby's, Texas Med Clinic, and CVS are good examples of Build-to-Suits. These can be built on a single lot or on a Pad site; a designated area in the shopping center. Typically, franchises have a very specific design and layout to which the Landlord has to build out. There would be a 15 year lease out for that property and usually require strong credentials to get approved. This is a great Investor purchase because of the ROI and strength of the Tenant.

THE LEASE AGREEMENT

The Lease Agreement itself also is derived from libraries.

Keep in mind that ownership and leasing differentiate with respect to right of use. If you own it, you can do whatever you want, update, landscaping, number of occupants (subject to ordinances and legality). When you lease, however, you are limited to what the Landlord allows and of course ordinances and legality, like renting a house.

Be cognizant that the Landlord has a responsibility to protect their property since it's their investment and if it is Multi-Tenant then they have to protect the other tenant's rights too. You can try to negotiate but there are some elements that just can't be value engineered. If you don't sign you don't get the lease.

If leasing is the right choice for you, here is the process.

THE LEASE AGREEMENT PROCESS

- Needs Assessment
- Tenant requirements: Size (sq. ft.), layout, location, parking, signage, budget.
- Landlord objectives: Desired tenant profile, lease length, rent structure, CAM (common area maintenance) recovery.
- Property Search & Tour
- Tenant (or Agent) identifies potential spaces.
- Tours scheduled to evaluate condition, layout, and amenities.
- Preliminary discussions on asking rent, concessions, and fit-out needs.
- Lease Drafting & Negotiation
- The Landlord or Leasing Agent will provide a proposal, known as the Letter of Intent (LOI). This will streamline the actual lease preparation and eventually the final Lease negation. Often goes through several rounds of revisions.
- Landlord's attorney drafts the lease.
- Tenant (and broker/attorney) reviews and negotiates:
- Rent structure (NNN, gross, modified gross)
- Responsibilities for repairs, insurance, utilities
- Use clause (permitted use, exclusivity rights)
- Assignment/subletting rules
- Termination & default remedies
- Due Diligence
- Tenant confirms zoning, permits, build-out feasibility.
- Landlord verifies tenant's financials and business history.
- Inspections may be done for HVAC, fire systems, etc.

- Final Lease Execution
- Both parties sign the lease agreement.
- Security deposit and first month's rent collected.
- Lease becomes binding.
- Build-Out & Pre-Occupancy
- Tenant begins improvements (TI) or landlord delivers space in agreed condition.
- Inspections and permitting as required.
- Certificate of Occupancy obtained.
- Move-In & Lease Management
- Tenant takes possession.
- Landlord begins ongoing property management, rent collection, and CAM reconciliation (if applicable).
- Both parties manage obligations until lease expiration.

QUICK REFERENCE TO COMMERCIAL REAL ESTATE CONTRACTS

- Commercial Real Estate Purchase/Sale Contracts
- Commercial Real Estate Contracts Checklist
- Basic Leasing Terms
- Lease Structures and Expenses
- Property Classifications
- The Lease Agreement
- The Lease Agreement Process

CHAPTER NINE

INVESTING & BUILDING

I say Investing rather than buying because you are investing into real estate when you buy, regardless of Owner or Non- Owner Occupied, rather than leasing. A business that is leasing is an investment, in the business sense but not into real estate. Whereas a business that buys its building for operations is both a business and a real estate investment.

I explain it this way because it is common to just say hey, I'll buy a property for my business whereas that might not be ideal. When you Invest in any real estate it comes with its own challenges, like capital or cash flow management, maintenance, taxes, and changing market, government, or economic changes. We have covered that. It takes time and money. Where do you want to put it? Let's review some cash flow or debt ideology.

You are likely schooled in the Robert Kiyosaki ideology. If not, I encourage you to read up on him. He believes that leveraging OPM is the key to maximizing ROI. Some people are very open to this; others are very hesitant to take on debt. Some of you are in the position of buying your property cash, but many are not. Let's talk about Robert's Good Debt. vs. Bad Debt ideology before we progress.

There may be a few Dave Ramsey fans reading my book so they may cringe at my Good Debt vs. Bad Debt discussion. Ramsey teaches that debt is immoral and names countless businesses that don't or have never used debt. In today's world that is not very common or possible, but also limits who can be Small Business Owners. Leverage allows more. I have read his book and yes, I am a Kiyosaki fan and not a Ramsey fan, but we do not all share the same values. You may want to read Financial IQ by Robert Kiyosaki to get a better handle on why Robert teaches a different approach and why I subscribe to the belief that leveraging is good. At the end of the day, you have to do what is right for you.

Businesses and real estate are two assets that you can control, unlike trading paper – stocks, mutual funds, and bonds, which are uncontrolled risk since you have no control over those business decisions or operations. No matter how much you diversify, your investment is controlled by other people. Diversification only manages risk; it doesn't control or eliminate it.

GOOD DEBT VS. BAD DEBT

Good Debt – The simple definition of good debt is that it builds wealth Leveraged by OPM.

Bad Debt – The simple definition of bad debt is that it consumes wealth.

Bad Debt includes consumer debt, automobiles, and everything that does not create positive cash flow such as vacations, furniture, automobiles, and yes, poor real estate investments.

I'm not going to go into depth about student loans since its off-topic and that I might end up in a rant about correlation vs. causation of college as it pertains to wealth building and success. I hold two higher education degrees and have student debt so I'm speaking from the heart and experience. This awareness also comes from understanding Macro Economics and Labor Force dynamics, but I digress. Send your letters to 1600 Pennsylvania Ave NW, Washington, DC 20500. Maybe they can fix the issue of why college is so expensive and why we seem to have to spend money for art history and P.E classes to learn engineering or business.

Kiyosaki receives disgruntled emails everyday about his remarks that your personal residence is not an investment. As a REALTOR I certainly understand it is almost sacrilegious to agree with him, but having studied business, investments, and holding two business degrees I do, mostly. It doesn't mean you shouldn't own a house, it just means it's not Good Debt and it should not be treated the same way as an investment like Multifamily or Commercial Real Estate. On that note, let's talk about how Kiyosaki handles these challenging situations personally.

Robert wanted to buy a Porche. He had the cash, of course. He discussed with his wife Kim, who said she had just one requirement – he had to find Good Debt to off-set the expense. While he intended to purchase it cash, he considered it Bad Debt since he expects his money to make money and the car is a consumer item, a personal expense, thus a consumer debt. He needed $150,000 to correct the problem. He called his gold broker and told him to do enough trading to make $150,000. With that he was able to pay for the Porsche, replenish his bank account with the cash expenditure, and cover the broker fee.

I know this scenario sounds unrealistic to most people, but focus on two key principles: (1) Good Debt creates wealth by leveraging OPM and (2) Stay in control your own money.

I love Robert's attitude. He realizes that the finer things in life are worth having and that we all deserve the right to own the many beautiful things that God has placed in our world – to the extent that we act as responsibly and be good stewards of money.

Borrowing from Kiyosaki's principles, there are four primary asset classes a person can invest: Businesses, Real estate, Paper assets (stocks and bonds), and Commodities (minerals and crypto). Most of these assets are difficult to leverage, but real estate is the exception. Lenders love to collateralize debt so they are happy to lend you money for a real estate transaction.

IMPROVED PROPERTIES VS. NEW CONSTRUCTION

Buying an existing building and **new construction** are two very different experiences — both in process and financing. The key distinction often depends on whether the existing property is turnkey or requires extensive renovation.

If the property is turnkey, the process is similar to buying a home. You make the purchase and then personalize it with cosmetic upgrades like paint, flooring, or other minor improvements.

Renovations can be one all at once or in phases, depending on your needs and available capital.

However, **if the property needs major repairs** — such as foundation work, full interior demolition, or new electrical systems — it will likely require short-term commercial construction financing, just like a ground-up build.

Even so, **don't overlook a property that checks most of your boxes**: location, parking, zoning, ceiling height — even if the layout doesn't initially fit your needs. A complete renovation may still be the smarter path. Starting with an existing structure often means key infrastructure — zoning, foundation, parking lots, and utilities — is already in place, which can make it more cost-effective than building from scratch.

Short-term commercial construction loans typically require that you pledge the land as collateral, and funds are disbursed in draws throughout the construction period. Once the project is complete and a Certificate of Occupancy is issued, the loan is converted (or refinanced) into a permanent commercial mortgage.

***TIP**: Whenever possible, look for one-time close financing rather than a double close — it helps minimize total closing costs and paperwork.*

PROPERTY MANAGEMENT

I recommend hiring a Property Manager. They have Facility Managers that are trained to identify issues and respond timely. Sure, you could do some of it yourself but are you in the real estate business or are you in the [your core business] business?

There is a second reason to hire a professional management firm. Just like renting houses, people don't always pay their rent on time. The last thing you need is your Tenant coming into your place of business to tell you they can't pay their rent or creates a disturbance. Perhaps they had a plumbing leak while you're in a meeting with a client, pull your receptionist away, or create a scene. It's worth the small price to pay to avoid the big price of costing you time and money. Hire a professionally property manager.

MAINTENANCE

Owning your business property is just like a house with the addition of collecting rents and being on a larger scale.

One of the critical decisions about buying verses leasing is the quality of Due Diligence required of a subject property to evaluate the full investment outlay. You may find that the property has deferred maintenance issues beyond the renovation you have in mind for operations and aesthetics.

The Commercial Property Condition Statement and a good inspection from a Licensed Real Estate Inspector is all good, but don't forget to check the Indoor Air Quality and do an Environmental Phase study to get the full picture; Due Diligence. Refer to Chapter 12 for EcoWise discussion. You may also want to request a repair history, warranties, and past insurance claims. It would also be prudent to get everything quoted during the Feasibility period.

KEY BUYER QUESTIONS FOR COMMERCIAL REAL ESTATE

1. What is the current occupancy and tenant profile?
2. What is the lease structure and remaining lease terms?
3. What is the property's current Net Operating Income (NOI)?
4. What is the Cap Rate and how does this property compare?
5. What are the operating expenses and who pays them?
6. What condition is the building in?
7. What is the zoning and permitted use?
8. What is the area's growth outlook and location dynamics?
9. Are there environmental issues or liabilities?
10. What is the financing and exit strategy potential?

QUICK REFERENCE TO INVESTING AND BUILDING

- Good Debt vs. Bad Debt
- Improved Properties versus New Construction
- Property Management
- Maintenance
- Key Buyer Questions for Commercial Real Estate

CHAPTER TEN

S.M.A.R.T. GOAL DECISION PLANNER

If you are not in the habit of writing goals this might be a good time to start so you can align your real estate decisions. I've created a decision model based on the S.M.A.R.T. goal system to guide Small Business Owners towards Smart Decisions.

Before I introduce my S.M.A.R.T. Decision Planner discussion, it might be helpful to know that I developed this to work with Small Business Owners to define your real estate needs. Everything up to now has been to prepare you for the transaction. This model is action based to start your strategy.

S.M.A.R.T GOAL DECISIONS

S.M.A.R.T goals are widely used in sales and management. The R seems to have different meanings by different people. I prefer that R = Relevant, but others say Results Oriented or Relational. If it isn't relevant to you or your situation, what is the point? You don't want to find yourself in an irrelevant property that is obsolete or doesn't meet your goals down for 1, 3, 5 or even 10 years. Let's review my S.M.A.R.T Decision Planner.

S.M.A.R.T. DECISION PLANNER

You may have heard of S.M.A.R.T Goals, so let's translate them into S.M.A.R.T Decisions. You're playing a game called Business and I am here to help you make S.M.A.R.T decisions to win the game. This diagram is just to give you a visual and not nearly the number of items to consider.

S

SPECIFIC

- I want to obtain a retail center within the next 6 months
- I want to build a retirement fund paying $10,000/mo from age 64-80
- I want to provide my services to at least 500 people /mo.

M

MEASUREABLE

- Can the goals be measured by money?
- Can the goals be measured by other means to track when achieved?

A

ATTAINABLE/ ACHIEVABLE

- Can I achieve these goals with respect to my resources and availability?
- Do I have access to the required capital?
- Do I personally have what it takes to do this?
- Does it fit my current and future needs?

R

RELEVANT

- Is this business model sustainable? For how long?
- Are there any market challenges with the economy or gov.?
- What do I hope to achieve with this?

T

TIMELY

- Can the goals be measured by time?
- Can the times be adjusted as needed?
- Can I still measure performance if I need to adjust?

S: SPECIFIC

Goals should be specific. Write as simplistic and clearly as you can to achieve what you want, specifically, the Ws: Who, What, When, and Why. I would also throw in the H, How.

M: MEASURABLE

Goals should be measurable. Usually, the entire goal statement is a measure for the project, but Key Performance Indicators (KPI) should also be considered.

A: ACHIEVABLE

Goals should be achievable; they should stretch you slightly so you feel challenged, but defined well enough so that you can achieve them. You must possess the appropriate knowledge, skills, and abilities needed to achieve the goal. You can meet most any goal when you plan your steps wisely and establish a timeframe that allows you to carry out those steps. As you carry out the steps, you can achieve goals that may have seemed impossible when you started. On the other hand, if a goal is impossible to achieve, you may not even try.

R: RELEVANT

Your decisions should fit into your business goals, personal goals, business culture, and possibly spiritual, given today's business environment and what is trending.

T: TIME-BOUND

Goals should be linked to a timeframe that creates a practical sense of urgency, or results in tension between the current reality and the vision of the goal. Without such tension, the goal is unlikely to produce a relevant outcome.

Here are some suggestions to help you brainstorm:

- Define your 3, 5, and 10 year property goals.
- Define your needs to include style, and vibe.
- Define your target market in terms of demographics, lifestyle, generational, trends, and Consumer Behavior.
- Define locations where your target market and your employee base live, works, and plays.
- Define your physical space and parking needs.
- Define your budget to lease, buy, or build.
- Define your timeline for achieving your goals.
- Determine if the property is achievable given current market conditions.
- Determine if the property is achievable given your current human and financial resources.
- Determine if the property is consistent with today's industry trends and flexible enough to be agile in the future.
- Determine if the property is a good fit for your personal goals.
- Develop a timeline to include a specific date to hire an Agent.
- Develop a timeline to include property search and research.
- Develop a timeline for property acquisition, build out, moving, marketing, and training.

I encourage you to brainstorm with your team, investor, family, and any accountability partners or advisors.

What Are Key Performance Indicators (KPIs)?

Key performance indicators (KPIs) are defined measurements used to assess a company's long-term performance. Organizations use KPIs to track their progress on key business objectives.

KPIs help a company achieve its strategic, financial, and operational goals, particularly when compared to those of other businesses within the same sector. They can also be used to judge progress or achievements against a set of benchmarks or past performance.

Key Takeaways

Key performance indicators (KPIs) measure a company's success vs. a set of targets, objectives, or industry peers.

KPIs can be financial, including net profit (or the bottom line, net income), revenues minus certain expenses, or the current ratio (liquidity and cash availability).

Customer-focused KPIs generally center on per-customer efficiency, customer satisfaction, and customer retention.

Process-focused KPIs aim to measure and monitor operational performance across the organization.

Businesses generally measure and track KPIs through analytics software and reporting tools.

CHAPTER ELEVEN

TIMEWISE PLANNER

Just like my S.M.A.R.T. Decision Planner, my TimeWise Planner is a great tool to help you, the Small Business Owner, to understand what to expect, how to budget time, and how the process works.

Your Agent should offer a time planning system to help you be efficient and effective with time. As Small Business Owners we wear many hats and it's easy for things to fall off your plate or get set aside. This is a streamlined guide to follow the process time and know what to expect.

If you are leasing the planner would be different. Go through my checklists or create your own to do a spreadsheet timeline. It is a great way to budget time and not miss key events. Here is an example.

TIMEWISE PLANNER

If you could wave a magic wand, when would you open your doors?

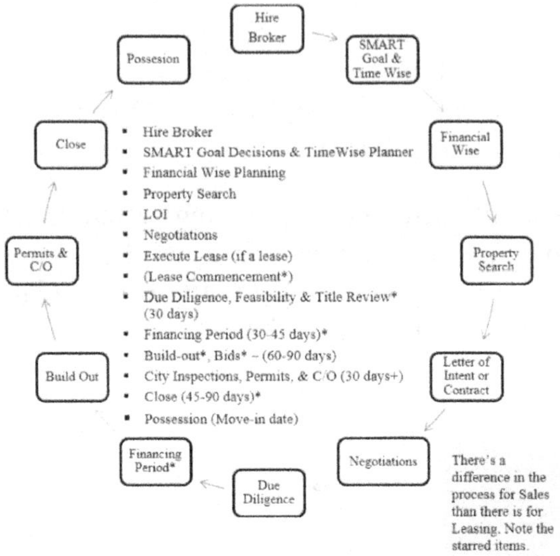

SAMPLE TIMEWISE PLANNER

CLIENT	Define End-User Centric Needs	
CLIENT	Define Property Centric Needs	
CLIENT	Create S.M.A.R.T Decision Planner	
CLIENT	Create TimeWise Planner	
CLIENT + LENDER	Create Financial Wise Planner	
CLIENT + AGENT	Hire you Agent	
CLIENT + AGENT	Pre-Acquisition Planning	2-6 months out
CLIENT + AGENT	Establish entity structure	30-120 days out
CLIENT + AGENT	Property Search & Initial Evaluation	
CLIENT + AGENT	Negotiations via LOI	
CLIENT + AGENT	Purchase & Sale Agreement	30 days out
CLIENT + AGENT	Due Diligence Period	30-90 days out
CLIENT + LENDER	Financing & Appraisal	30 days out
CLIENT + AGENT	Closing Preparation	1 week out
CLIENT + AGENT	Closing	
CLIENT + AGENT	Take possession and enjoy	
CLIENT + AGENT	Post-Closing	

CHAPTER TWELVE

ECOWISE DECISIONS

Formerly known as Green Commercial Realty, now Criado Realty, I approach real estate with green in mind – money, efficiency, and environmental. Green really is the catchy term for what is environmental building science. It's everywhere – events, businesses, and the news. However, ask anyone to define green and you'll get a variety of answers. In 2025, President Trump threw out the Green Initiative which funded many green building technologies, but I have to say that even though I try to minimize my global footprint, I am glad the funding for windfarms will as they are dominating the Texas coast and you see them all over North Shore Hawaii killing rare birds and wildlife. I will agree that the climate experiment since former President Al Gore began his push, that much of it has been unproven. But for many, like the Girl Scout in me, I still want to do my part to be environmentally responsible. There are many very valuable and economically sound aspects to incorporate.

Take from this what is important to you. The rest can be fire starter in your camp fire. Wait, if you are not a Girl or Boy Scout and don't love camping you might not be doing that. I know that emojis and LOL isn't acceptable to insert into a book but, LOL and ☺!

As a Certified EcoBroker and NAR GREEN Broker I define green to mean energy efficiency, environmental responsibility, and healthy indoor air quality.

MY E3 BUSINESS MODEL

ECOLOGY, EFFICIENCY, AND ECONOMICS

ECOLOGY. EFFICIENCY. ECONOMICS.

ECOLOGY FOR THE BUSINESS – Being a good steward of the earth means intentionally reducing and reusing natural resources while choosing materials that minimize off-gassing and environmental impact. This approach not only supports a healthier planet but also promotes healthier living and working environments.

Here are some **practical, ecology-minded ways** a business can improve the employee working environment—focusing on **health, happiness, and sustainability** ☘

- **Introduce Biophilic Design**
  Incorporate plants, green walls, or natural light to reconnect employees with nature. Research shows biophilic design lowers stress, improves concentration, and increases overall workplace satisfaction.

- **Improve Air Quality**
  Use air-purifying plants, open windows regularly, and maintain HVAC systems with eco-friendly filters. Clean indoor air reduces headaches, fatigue, and absenteeism.

- **Encourage Active Transportation**
  Provide bike racks, showers, and incentives for walking, biking, or using public transport. This promotes fitness while reducing the company's carbon footprint.

- **Create a Green Workspace Policy**
  Reduce waste through recycling stations, composting bins, and refillable water stations. Encourage digital rather than printed documents and reward eco-friendly habits.

- **Optimize Natural Light and Ergonomics**
  Design workspaces that maximize sunlight and use energy-efficient LED lighting. Pair that with ergonomic furniture to support physical comfort and posture health.

- **Offer Mindfulness & Wellness Programs**
  Host yoga, meditation, or breathing-technique sessions. These reduce stress and build community while improving mental resilience.

- **Introduce Eco-Friendly Office Supplies**
  Switch to recycled materials and biodegradable cleaning products. Align purchasing decisions with environmental responsibility.

- **Build Quiet and Relaxation Zones**
  Create spaces for employees to recharge—quiet pods, outdoor seating areas, or mini Zen gardens. A short break in a calm environment enhances focus and creativity.

- **Promote Healthy Food & Hydration**
  Provide filtered water, fruit bowls, or partner with local vendors offering healthy, sustainable snacks. Consider Meatless Mondays or local farm partnerships.

- **Celebrate Green Initiatives Together**
  Organize volunteer clean-ups, community garden days, or sustainability challenges. Collective participation boosts morale and shared purpose.

- **Flexible & Remote Work Options**
  Allow hybrid schedules and digital collaboration to reduce commuting pollution while improving work-life balance and overall happiness.

- **Measure and Share Impact**
  Track sustainability metrics (waste reduction, energy savings, wellness participation) and celebrate progress publicly—transparency builds pride and accountability.

Do you want to know more? Find great blogs like "Detox Your Work Environment to Increase Your Bottom Line"

EFFICIENCY IN THE BUSINESS – Reduce consumption and eliminate waste. "Waste not, want not" is more than a saying—it's a strategy for saving money, optimizing resources, and acting responsibly toward the environment.

ECONOMICS FOR THE BUSINESS – By being socially and economically relevant you can position your company with a competitive advantage.

A brief comment on Indoor Air Quality. *I may not know what bad air looks like but when I see it, I know it's there.*

It's not always as obvious as that. It often smells ever so faintly or results in dust on your desk that is harming your pulmonary and can even sometimes hospitalize you and your employees. Don't forget to comply with OSHA (Occupational Safety and Health Administration). This is not a greenie beanie idea! OSHA compliance is important and is something that every business needs to know.

GREEN FEATURES AND BENEFITS BY BUILDERS

Essentially, Green building is better quality because the first rule is to "tighten the envelope." This means no gaps, which starts with cutting straight, and not being wasteful with materials resulting in less energy waste, saving money. It goes much deeper by using re-purposed materials, recycling waste, and minimizing off-gassing from VOCs (Volatile Organic Chemicals). Even with today's changing ideology about climate control, saving energy and reducing chemical output has financial savings impact.

Here are some considerations:

Energy Efficiency. Even with alternative it's important not to waste. Saves you money on utilities. In the South and West, HVAC and water heaters account for most of the utility bill. **Tighten the Envelope**. Did you feel a draft? **Duct Blast Tests**. This Measures tightness of the building envelope. **Insulation.** Spray foam, radiant barrier roofing, and Cellulose insulation are better insulations choices than fiberglass. This too helps you save money but also creates a more comfortable environment. Who wants cold in the winter and hot in the summer?

Renewable energy. There are so many options now including clean coal and other forms. I used to be a proponent of solar, and still am for personal camping or solar roofing, but not so keen on wind farms. If you have driven in windfarm areas you know what I mean. Where do they bury those dead windmills anyway? They cannot be recycled.

Rain water harvesting. There are pros and cons with this and some states or cities have policies against it. If you take the rain water you may be affecting the environment in other ways. I like how the City of San Antonio saves us money by using captured gray water (non-potable) water to water all the plants on the San Antonio River Walk. It saves you money on water bills & in this case, also on water processing.

Design principles. For example, create comfort and save money by optimizing energy. Use Low E windows and orient for energy efficiency (in South Texas), position the longest side facing north-south to minimize east-west sun exposure and maximize passive solar heating from the south. This strategy limits the amount of direct sun hitting the house during the hottest parts of the day, which reduces cooling costs, while allowing the south side to receive ample sunlight during winter months for warmth. Other key strategies include designing for natural airflow, strategic window placement, and using high-R-value insulation and other building envelope materials.

Avoid VOCs (Volatile Organic Chemicals). VOCs vaporize (become a gas) at room temperature. VOC are the leading cause of ground-level ozone (air pollution, also known as "smog"). Common sources which may emit VOC into the air include housekeeping and maintenance products; paints, coatings, and inks; and building and furnishing materials. (EPA)

Repurposing buildings. I was just reading a LinkedIn post where Chick-fila bought a CVS that closed because of its location. They aren't going to tear it down; they are going to rehab it. Emoji time, very cool!

Used vs New. Buying used is sometimes cheaper or more interesting than buying new. Or you can obtain what you thought you couldn't since cities sprawl out.

Repurposing "Brownfields." A brownfield is a parcel or property that has been deemed hazardous and needs remediation. To build, expand, redevelop, or reuse may be complicated by the presence or potential presence of a hazardous substance, pollutant, or contaminant. Don't rule it out. Talk to an engineer. You may find it is the better value or serves your purpose better. Tax Benefits - There are city and sometime state or federal tax incentives to remediate properties or build in older areas to gentrify the area. In San Antonio we have a IDZ zoning to spur growth I an area. Infill Development Zone. Rehabs in older areas also have tax benefits. Due Diligence.

GREEN LEADERSHIP ORGANIZATIONS

In 2007 I came across an entity called US Green Builders Association (LEED program) and began to understand the trend toward green. Later when I decided to become an independent real estate broker, I discovered two other entities: BSAG and GREEN. They exist to avoid "Green washing" by setting standards for green, aka Environmental Building Science. As mentioned earlier, I am certified by two entities so let's talk about them and a few others.

LEADERSHIP IN ENERGY AND ENVIRONMENTAL DESIGN

The (LEED) is a program that provides third-party verification of green buildings. The LEED rating systems address a wide variety of buildings types, including commercial buildings, homes, neighborhoods, retail, healthcare, and schools, as well as every phase of the building lifecycle including design, construction, operations, and maintenance. Development of LEED began in 1993, spearheaded by Natural Resources Defense Council (NRDC) senior scientist Robert K. Watson.

ECOBROKER

The EcoBroker designation is an environmental and energy education program for real estate professionals, awarded by the Association of Energy and Environment Real Estate Professionals. Founded by John Beldock in 2002, CEO of EcoBroker International, Energy Solutions Lead and Director at AI Data Center Power and Finance Solutions, Author, Educator, Team Builder, Real Estate Licensee. Serving public and private sectors since 1982.

NAR GREEN

GREEN is the only designation approved by the National Association of Realtors (NAR). The program was developed in 2008 by the Real Estate Buyer's Agent Council of NAR, with administration transferred to the Green Resource Council.

BUILD SAN ANTONIO GREEN (BSAG)

San Antonio has some practical and interesting green initiatives that save money and eliminate waste. It's a nationally recognized non-profit organization that exists to create sustainable housing. Upon discovering this entity, I created my company with a green emphasis. I am the only non-builder company that has won a BSAG award. It was for the support and initiatives towards environmental stewardship. I have since re-branded but still hold these principles dear. I am just more pragmatic about it, mostly.

I was particularly honored by the award given the kind words Mr. William R Sinkin, the founder, said when he learned what I do for the community. He pulled me aside from an outdoor Build San Antonio Green event to go for a short walk to hear about his vision. Additionally, I am proud of my heritage – Tex-Mex-Chinese American and that the foundation that financed the BSAG launch included the Hispanic Urban Development division of HUD.

I have always found that indigenous people are more connected with ecology and the environment. I say Mex but my ancestry goes back to Mesoamerican i.e. Aztec, Maya, Toltec, and Olmec. Having lived in Hawaii for many years I can attest to that with the indigenous Hawaiian people, with whom too I affiliate and respect the love of the 'Aina. *"Land," but more profoundly, it signifies that which feeds and sustains life.*

I invite you to explore The William R. Sinkin Eco Centro, a community outreach center for environmental sustainability operated by Alamo Colleges. It's located at San Antonio College, 1819 N. Main Ave, San Antonio, TX 78212 ▯ (210) 486-0417

The LEED-certified, 3,000+ square foot facility serves as an example of sustainable building with a solar-photovoltaic system connected to 135 roof-mounted solar panels, a 2,700-gallon water catchment tank and five 40-gallon tanks, water-wise landscaping, four electric vehicle charging stations, and large composting and gardening areas.

What is Build San Antonio Green?

"It is San Antonio's National Award-winning Green Building Program. As a voluntary, third-party certification program, we work with the homebuilding community to help create homes with increased efficiency, comfort, and durability. Programs include Single Family New Construction, Historic Retrofits, and Multifamily Projects."

BSAG Mission

The mission of BSAG is to protect and enhance the quality of life of the citizens of the metropolitan San Antonio Area by developing standards by which to certify newly constructed and existing structures to green standards, and to provide leadership, expertise, and education for the wise, efficient, and sustainable use of energy and resources.

QUICK REFERENCE TO BUYING AND BUILDING

- e3 Business Model
- Green Features & Benefits
- Green Leadership Organizations
- Leadership in Energy and Environmental Design
- EcoBroker
- NAR GREEN
- Build San Antonio Green

ABOUT THE AUTHOR

Cathy Criado is a Licensed Real Estate Broker based in San Antonio, Texas, and a multi-million-dollar producer in both commercial and residential real estate. She earned her M.B.A. from the University of Texas at San Antonio and a BB.A. from the University of Texas at Arlington. Beyond real estate, she is a Business Consultant and active community member, having served on the San Antonio Board of Realtors Public Policy Committee, the Alamo Heights Chamber of Commerce, and the Girl Scouts of Southwest Texas council—where she sat on the renaming board uniting four regional councils across West and South Texas.

Cathy continues to lend her time and expertise to a variety of boards and initiatives, including SAWS' water conservation and waste management programs, La Prensa fundraising efforts, and other ad hoc community projects.

Before becoming an author, Cathy was already a storyteller, blogger, and consultant—someone who loved helping people make sense of complex ideas. *Are You Ready for Commercial Real Estate?* became the first of several books she plans to write because it lays the foundation for everything she's learned: combining years of experience, real-world client stories, and business principles to truly help others make informed decisions.

As a military dependent, Cathy has traveled to four continents and lived in Hawaii, experiences that shaped her love of culture and people. She enjoys gourmet cooking, art, hula and salsa dancing, jazz, blues, and alternative rock. Above all, she cherishes time spent with her family, friends, and her loyal dog, Leonard.

12 FAVORITE BUSINESS BOOKS

1. The Greatest Salesman in the World – OG Mandino
2. Rich Dad Poor Dad's Financial IQ – Robert Kiyosaki
3. Rich Dad Poor Dad's Cash Flow Quadrant – Robert Kiyosaki
4. The 10X Rule – Grant Cardone
5. Think & Grow Rich – Napolean Hill
6. Good to Great – Jim Collins
7. Eat Mo Chicken – S. Truett Cathy
8. More Than a Hobby – David Green
9. The Dip – Seth Godin
10. The Self-Directed IRA - Matt Sorensen
11. Master the Money Game – Tony Robbins
12. The Miracle Morning – Hal Elrod

Made in the USA
Monee, IL
04 November 2026

67386422R00059